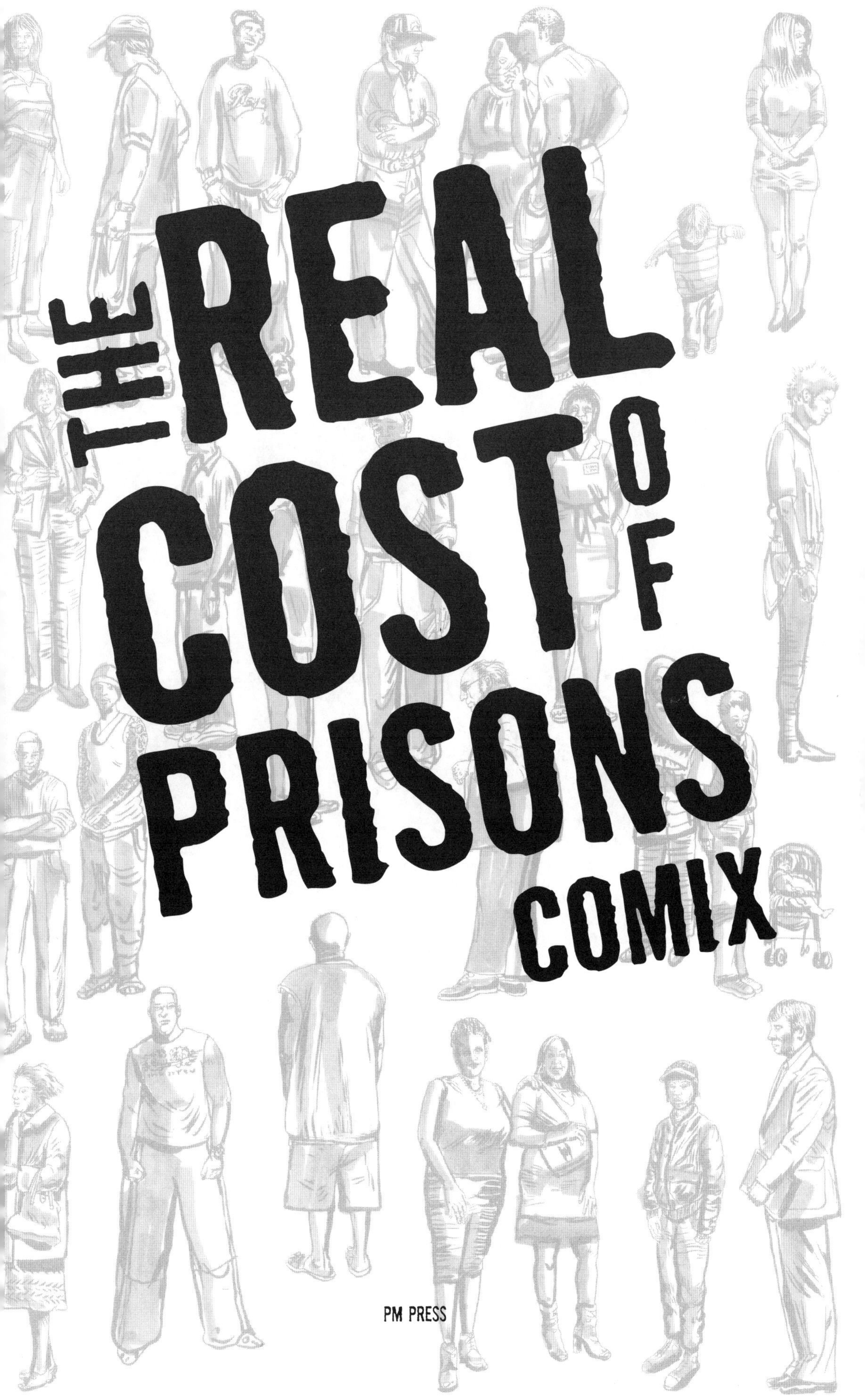

THE REAL COST OF PRISONS COMIX

PM PRESS

The Real Cost Of Prisons Comix
By Lois Ahrens

Cover design by Kevin Pyle
Cover illustration by Susan Willmarth
Layout and design by Courtney Utt

Published by:
PM Press
PO Box 23912
Oakland, CA 94623
www.pmpress.org

ISBN: 978-1-60486-034-4
Library Of Congress Control Number: 2008929092

10 9 8 7 6 5 4 3

Printed by the Employee Owners of Thomson-Shore in Dexter, Michigan.
www.thomsonshore.com
Printed in the USA on recycled paper.

This book is dedicated to all who are outraged by injustice

table of contents

preface

Comic books and anti-prison agitation and education may seem like an unlikely match, but it seemed perfect to me. My idea was to make comic books combining drawings and plain language to explain complex ideas and concepts. I wanted them to incorporate statistics, new research and footnotes but not scare off readers who were not used to reading academic articles and books. To do this, they needed to be about people's lives. The glossy cover would be attractive enough for someone doing laundry in a laundromat to pick one up and start reading.

The inspiration for the comic books came from three sources. For more than 30 years, I traveled to Mexico, where I saw women tending market stalls and sitting on park benches engrossed in photo novellas, or "picture stories." Photo novellas were everywhere, inexpensive to produce and buy. Only rarely do they have one reader.

In 2000, trade union leaders from South Africa's COSATU (The Congress of South African Trade Unions) gave me copies of two newly published, eye-opening publications: "Stop Privatisation" and "A South African Workers' Guide to Globalization." Using graphics, photos and concise explanations, they had created popular education materials which communicated complex ideas in easy-to-understand language. Their target audience was South African trade unionists, astute in political consciousness but perhaps without a lot of formal education.

Lastly, *A Field Guide to the U.S. Economy* written by economists James Heintz and Nancy Folbre used everyday language, graphs and cartoons to explain how the economy works. The book was written to help illuminate the complexities of economics for people with little or no background in economics.

My goal was to create materials which organizers, educators, medical and mental health providers, along with people directly experiencing the impact of mass incarceration could use in their work. It was the combination of the *Field Guide*, COSATU's publications and the photo novellas that led me to comic books.

The comic books are one part of The Real Cost of Prisons Project (RCPP), which began in 2000. Many of the first people working with the RCPP were economists. They brought to the Project their social, economic and political analysis of how we had come to this terrible place where imprisonment had spiraled into mass incarceration.

WHAT DRIVES MASS INCARCERATION?

Every year from 1947 through the beginning of the 1970s, approximately 200,000 people were incarcerated in the U.S. Today there are more than 2.3 million men and women incarcerated with more than 5 million more on parole and probation—one in every 32 adults.

In our analysis of mass incarceration, we did not seek to remove individual responsibility; however, we wanted to place an individual within a bigger picture. To do this we began by describing how Ronald Reagan and the neoliberal agenda came to power in 1980 by using covert and overt racist messages fabricating the myth of the welfare queen, capitalizing on fears of affirmative action and the gains made in the civil rights movement of 1950s and 60s, fostering alarm about crime to exploit the divisions between poor and working-class whites and African Americans which remain today. The racist sub-text of neo-liberal political campaigns succeeded in creating acceptance of mass incarceration while simultaneously capitalizing on the industries they created to police, prosecute, cage and control millions of people.

Neo-liberal policies have been in place for almost thirty years. As a result many people are not aware that our political and economic life now is not the result of natural course of events but rather of a systemically created ideology that has pervaded every aspect of our daily lives. Deregulation and globalization—loss of U.S. manufacturing, outsourcing; corporate agriculture and the disappearance of the family farm; reduction of protections for workers; decrease in number of unionized workers; privatization of hospitals, water, education, prisons and the military; drastic cuts in public spending for welfare, public schools, public transportation, housing and job training; and attacks on affirmative action—are now part of the air we breathe. These policies have resulted in impoverishing urban economies, limiting opportunities for meaningful work and slashing funding for quality education, marginalizing the poor, and creating more inequality.

The comic books place individual experience in this context and challenge a central message of neo-liberal ideology: the myth that people can pull themselves up by their own bootstraps. In this paradigm, racism, sexism, classism and economic inequality are not part of the picture. Most people now believe that change happens through personal transformation rather than political struggle and change.

A central goal of the comic books is to politicize, not pathologize. Despite years of conditioning, our message appears to be welcome. As of this writing 125,000 comic books have been printed. More than 100,000 have been sent free of charge.

When we fill requests for comic books, we generally send all three. We do this to encourage organizers to think and act across issue areas by providing a basic resource with which they can begin to forge coalitions. The movement to end mass incarceration will be strengthened when activists working to stop the building of new prisons and jails include activists working to end mandatory minimum drug sentences. It is equally important for people organizing to change sentencing policy to understand the rudiments of the financing and siting of prisons and jails. Every program and project is strengthened by not marginalizing women and by educating about how racism and classism continue to drive incarceration. In this way, we seek to break down some of the boundaries that hinder the movement for justice.

FROM SECOND CHANCE TATTOO REMOVAL TO THE YAKIMA RESERVATION SCHOOL

Many thousands of comic books are being used by programs working with youth. Some examples include: NY Correctional Association's Juvenile Justice Project "Each One, Teach One"; Homies Organizing the Mission to Empower Youth for workshops on incarceration in two primarily Latino high schools in San Francisco; Children's Aid Society, NY, for a youth reentry program from Riker's Island in Brooklyn, the Bronx and Manhattan; Cibecue High School on the White Mountain Apache Indian Reservation in East Central Arizona; Central Juvenile Hall in Los Angeles; Partners In Health Program in Dorchester, MA; Second Chance Tattoo Removal in San Francisco for youth and former gang members; Yakima Indian Reservation School, Wapato, WA; a comic book project for youth in the Milwaukee schools and one at the Heritage School in Manhattan; a high school anti-violence campaign in Philadelphia; and Young Women's Empowerment workshops in Chicago.

Thousands more have been used by health educators and providers, including training for rural health students and their preceptors in West Virginia; classes for midwives and nurses;

support groups for drug users in programs throughout the country; clients and staff at AIDS Action Committee in Boston; an HIV and Hepatitis C prevention project in 14 counties in northeast Alabama; for work with youth as part of a wellness coalition at the Railbelt Mental Health and Addiction Program in Nenana, Alaska; in an STD/AIDS prevention program in San Diego; for participants in the National Summit to Ensure the Health and Humanity of Pregnant and Birthing Women; and for the training of doulas in Washington State.

Hundreds of organizations, big and small, are using the comic books in workshops, outreach and organizing. A sample includes A New Way of Life, LA; Alabama Drug Policy Alliance; CLAIM, Chicago; Critical Resistance; National CURE and many CURE chapters; Education Not Incarceration, Berkeley; Ella Baker Center for Human Rights, Oakland, CA; Families to Amend California's Three Strikes (FACTS); Federation of Child Care Centers of Alabama; Fortune Society, NY; Getting Out and Staying Out, NY; Highlander Center, New Market, TN; The StopMax Campaign; Informed Citizens for a Better North Country, Milan, NH; Justice Now! Oakland, CA; Journey for Justice, Montgomery, AL; Legal Services for Prisoners with Children, San Francisco; Missouri NAACP Prison Project; The Osborne Association, NY; Private Corrections Institute; Sex Workers Organizing Project, AZ; South Texans Opposing Private Prisons, Laredo, TX; Students for a Sensible Drug Policy; Time for Change Foundation, San Bernardino, CA; Unity Radio Broadcasting Project, Syracuse, NY and the Welfare Rights Coalition, Olympia, WA.

COMIC BOOKS ON CHURCH PEWS

Prison politicizes many prisoners. Some prisoners are fortunate to have families and support systems that provide magazine subscriptions and send books and newspaper articles; however, in this age of information overload in the "free world," politically conscious prisoners are often starved for information, new research and political material. Unfortunately many organizations have stopped printing hard copies of their reports, fact sheets and resources. More and more, research important to prisoners is available only on websites, making it almost impossible for prisoners to have access to current, relevant materials they can use in their continuing education and in organizing work inside of prisons. The comic books reflect the lives of many prisoners and speak to their experience, and are free and available. Comic books have been received by prisoners in every state prison system, every federal prison and numerous jails. Thousands more have been sent to prisoners through 13 Books Through Bars organizations. We know that comic books are passed hand to hand by prisoners, since as soon as a set is sent to one prisoner, not a week passes before we begin receiving requests from other prisoners at that prison. Word of the comic books spreads from prisoners to their families, friends and organizations with which they work, and the network continues to expand. One prisoner wrote that he found one on a pew in the prison chapel.

In response to the comic books, we began to receive a wealth of insightful political writing and comix from prisoners. This inspired us to create two sections of The Real Cost of Prisons website: *Writing from Prison* and *Comix from Inside*. The comic books have put us in touch with hundreds of politicized prisoners. Thanks to them, we have become more involved in organizing against the cruelties of life without parole, juvenile life without parole, supermax prisons, intensive management units and other forms of segregation.

Poster-sized comic book pages have been used in exhibits around the country and tacked to walls in offices everywhere. Individual pages are incorporated into leaflets and reproduced in newsletters. The comic books have been downloaded from the website more than 2,000 times a year.

A ONE-WEEK PROJECT GROWS INTO EIGHT YEARS OF AGITATION, EDUCATION AND MORE

The publication of this book represents another step forward in a project which began in 2000. It was then I proposed the idea of a series of presentations by prison/justice activists as part of the Center for Popular Economics (CPE) Summer Institute which was to take place in July 2001. I named the course "The Real Cost of Prisons: Human, Economic and Social" and began researching presenters.

One of the first people I contacted was Ellen Miller-Mack, a nurse practitioner and anti-prison activist. She was organizing "Re-Claiming Our Lives," a one-day conference in Springfield, Massachusetts, focusing on women and incarceration. I called her to talk about the conference. I learned that she had been providing health care first to HIV+ men and then to women at the Hampden County jail on behalf of Brightwood Health Center. Our work together began and soon Ellen and I became a couple. When it was possible for us to marry in Massachusetts we did, in September 2004. Ellen is the author of two of the comic books in this book. She was a guiding force in the creation of two Real Cost of Prisons workshops on the ravages of drug policy and its devastating impact on women who are addicts. She has worked to ground the RCPP in her experience in "the trenches" and in her belief in the principles and practice of harm reduction. Ellen's participation has added soul to the Project and resonance for people who live the pain of the real cost of prisons.

I continued my search for presenters whose work combined research and activism. I found Tracy Huling, a filmmaker and independent researcher, and Jenni Gainsborough, then of The Sentencing Project. Both accepted invitations to attend the Summer Institute. They agreed to continue discussion on expanding the week-long session into something more long-lasting.

Soon after the Summer Institute ended, I asked key justice/policy activists if they would lend their names to a funding proposal I was writing to the Open Society Institute (OSI). An introduction from Tracy Huling to Helena Huang of OSI's Criminal Justice Initiative was invaluable. Helena Huang and OSI took a leap of faith in funding the Project. OSI supported our idea that activists need to learn from the experience of others, discover and incorporate new research into their work, take time to make connections across issue areas and deepen their analysis in order to become more effective organizers. In July 2002, a year after the Summer Institute, they funded the Project.

The Real Cost of Prisons Project was to last for two years. In that time three political economists and a group of advisors would create three workshops: "The Economics of Women and Families in the Criminal Justice System," "The Economics of the War on Drugs" and the "Federal, State and Private Financing of Prisons." We proposed teaching the workshops in six cities to activists and organizers. We also would create popular education materials based on the workshops and construct a website.

CPE economists James Heintz, Kiaran Honderich, Mark Brenner and early on, Geert Dhondt joined the team. Nine months into the project, I had the good fortune of meeting Craig Gilmore, who replaced Geert. Craig, who is the co-founder of the California Prison Moratorium Project, developed "The Real Cost of Financing and Siting of Prisons" workshop.

Soon after The Real Cost of Prisons Project grant was awarded to the Center for Popular Economics, the CPE Steering Committee unexpectedly decided they did not have the expertise to supervise me, a non-academic and a non-economist. OSI was open to another non-profit sponsor for the project. I contacted Marc Mauer and Malcolm Young, founder and then Executive Director of the Sentencing Project. They responded quickly and enthusiastically. Through the leadership of Malcolm and Marc, The Sentencing Project agreed to be the non-profit sponsor of The Real Cost of Prisons Project.

Finally we were underway. After a year of research, writing, long meetings and discussions with Mark Brenner, Craig Gilmore, Kiaran

Honderich, James Heintz and Ellen Miller-Mack, we began conducting trial runs of the workshops in Springfield, Massachusetts. The feedback we received was crucial to honing the content and the analysis of the workshops. For example, workshop participants told us it was essential to include alternative solutions and organizing successes to balance the stark reality we were presenting, otherwise we would run the risk of overwhelming people with the enormity of the work ahead.

After the first few workshops, we realized our target group of participants was too narrow and that we should include people and communities most egregiously affected by mass incarceration. Clearly three trainers were too few. We needed to train trainers to expand our base and geographical reach. In October 2004, James, Mark, Craig, Kiaran and I held a Train the Trainers workshop. Twenty-nine people attended from around the country. All were prison/justice activists, nine people had been incarcerated, three quarters of those attending were people of color and the age range was from 19 to 63. It was a powerful group. Each person was trained to teach one workshop, incorporating his or her own experience and insight. Many who attended remain connected to the RCPP, teaching workshops and grounding our work in the richness of their daily experience.

A COMIC BOOK NEOPHYTE PUBLISHES THREE COMIC BOOKS

With the Train the Trainers workshop completed, I shifted focus to the comic books. In January 2005, I read an article about someone writing a book about Will Eisner, the acclaimed comic book artist. That person was N Christopher Couch, who was teaching at the University of Massachusetts at Amherst, 30 minutes from where I live. We met and had a long talk. Chris suggested I contact Sabrina Jones, whom he thought might be interested in the project. Ellen and I went to New York to meet with Sabrina to talk about ideas for

Prisoners of the War on Drugs. We were so excited about her work and her ideas, that we hired her on the spot. Ellen would write the stories. I would do the research and help shape the content. Chris Shadoian was hired to layout and design the comic books.

At that meeting, Sabrina recommended Kevin Pyle, another artist with whom she works on the *World War 3 Illustrated* comic book series. I looked at Kevin's excellent work online and hoped he would agree to work with Craig Gilmore to create the comic book on financing and siting of prisons. Kevin and Craig formed a great team. Once again, my role was to provide editorial oversight. *Prison Town* was the first comic book released, in early March 2005, with 7500 copies printed. In April, *Prisoners of the War on Drugs* was published.

Ellen wrote the stories for *Prisoners of a Hard Life* and *Prisoners of the War on Drugs*, based on our research and on her years of experience providing health care on behalf of her health center to women at the Hampden County jail. The stories in *Prisoners of the War on Drugs* and *Prisoners of a Hard Life* are fictional but represent the lives of hundreds of thousands of people suffering as a result of the War on Drugs. Two stories are true. In *Prisoners of a Hard Life*, Regina McKnight's ordeal ends with her imprisonment in South Carolina. In an important ruling, on May 12, 2008 after 8 long years, the South Carolina Supreme Court reversed the 20-year homicide conviction of Regina McKnight. The unanimous decision recognized that research linking cocaine to stillbirths is based on outdated and inaccurate medical information. On June 19, 2008, she was freed. And, in "3 Strikes You're Out" in *Prisoners of the War in Drugs*, we describe what happened to Shane Reams and his mother, Sue. I thank them all for allowing their heartbreaking stories to be included in the comic books and this book.

Susan Willmarth, also a *World War 3 Illustrated* artist, enthusiastically signed on to do *Prisoners of a Hard Life*. Ellen and I met Susan in Great Barrington, Massachusetts, and talked for hours. Soon she began faxing us the powerful drawings that make up *Prisoners of a Hard*

Life—Women and Their Children, which was published in July 2005.

The work of these three talented, smart, politically committed artists—Kevin Pyle, Sabrina Jones and Susan Willmarth—continues to resonate emotionally and intellectually with tens of thousands of our readers. Our collaboration continues with the publication of this book. Susan did the artwork on the cover; Kevin is the art director and cover designer.

In the first month of publication, half the comic books we had printed were sent to organizations around the country. The comic books were flying out the door. I approached OSI seeking additional money to reprint the comic books and pay for postage. OSI funded the reprinting of *Prison Town* and increased the number of copies of the first printings of *Prisoners of the War on Drugs* and *Prisoners of a Hard Life*.

In November 2005, less than a year after the comic books were published, our supply had dwindled to almost nothing. Allan Clear of the Harm Reduction Coalition and Lynn Paltrow of National Advocates for Pregnant Women encouraged Michelle Coffey of the Starry Night Fund of the Tides Foundation to invite me to submit a grant to reprint and distribute the comic books. Thanks to Allan and Lynn's intervention, we were awarded our first grant from the Starry Night Fund. A second grant for reprinting and distribution was received from the Starry Night Fund in September 2006.

With the success of the comic books, I began receiving suggestions for new comic books. Suggestions included comic books focused on the criminalization and incarceration of youth, solitary confinement and control units, felony disenfranchisement, immigration detention and the obstacles men and women who have been incarcerated faced after being released from prison and jail. Many people have requested Spanish language-versions of the comic books. I had mistakenly thought that the demand and the apparent usefulness of the comic books would generate funding for new ones. Unfortunately this has not been the case. Instead, The Real Cost of Prisons Project including the workshops, our Train the Trainers program,

the website and news blog and the printing and distribution of free comic books are all unfunded despite numerous requests. The work continues but no new comic books have been created and in the near future the supply will run out.

A NATION-WIDE COMMUNITY OF ACTIVISTS FOR JUSTICE

The research of many people and organizations has been integral to the creation of the comic books and this book. Among them are Joanne Archibald, Mark Brenner, Eric Cadora, Todd Clear, Ruth Wilson Gilmore, Judith Green, James Heintz, Tracy Huling, Kiaran Honderich, Dana Kaplan, Marc Mauer, Lynn Paltrow, Tina Reynolds, Dina Rose and Peter Wagner. Organizations whose research we have drawn from include Families to Amend California's Three Shrikes (FACTS), Families Against Mandatory Minimums (FAMM), The Harm Reduction Coalition, National Advocates for Pregnant Women, The Prison Policy Initiative, The Sentencing Project, The Women's Prison Association, and others.

Over the years the Real Cost of Prisons website has become central to the Project. Mark Brenner created the original site. Soon after, Winston Close redesigned it and continues as webmaster, keeping it current and easy to use for more than 100,000 real page views per month. The website includes up-to-date research, books, and links to hundreds of organizations, PDFs of RCPP-created materials, including the three comic books, political and analytical comix and writing from prisoners, and a daily blog of news focusing on mass incarceration. (www.realcostofprisons.org/blog/).

Revan Schendler volunteered her editorial expertise and political insights just when I needed them. Ramsey Kanaan, publisher of PM Press, contacted me on December 24th, 2007 when we may have been the only two people at work, and asked if I was interested in anthologizing the comic books. Since then Ramsey and co-founder of PM Press, Craig O'Hara, have been enthusiastically involved in all aspects of the publication of this book. Courtney Utt has transformed the many parts she was given into an excellently designed book.

Tracy Huling began as my guide into the world of prison activism and research. She instantly understood the driving principles of The Real Cost of Prisons Project. Tracy continues to be an advisor and a friend. Craig Gilmore, who despite geographical distance, jumped into the void to create the Financing and Siting workshop, co-authored *Prison Town*, periodically teaches RCPP workshops and is there to provide incisive and often humorous take on the Kafkaesque world of California prisons. He and Ruthie Gilmore have generously written the introduction for this book.

Tiyo Attallah Salah-El, "caged" as he says, is life-sentenced in Dallas, Pennsylvania, since 1977. He is a teacher and prison abolitionist. Tiyo, like so many incarcerated men and women, is an insightful commentator of the ravages of mass incarceration both in and out of prison. Despite living in a system designed to denigrate, dehumanize and destroy, Tiyo, born in 1932, continues to devise and sustain educational programs for hundreds of his fellow prisoners, write and publish about prison abolition, and bring his ideas and spirit to his many fortunate friends, of which I am one.

Every day, my political and personal life is enriched by prisoners with whom I correspond and through my work with grassroots, family-based prison activists around the country. Comments from some of them are included in this book. They inspire my work to abolish prisons.

introduction

WHY THE REAL COST OF PRISONS MATTERS

RUTH WILSON GILMORE AND CRAIG GILMORE

What does it cost to lock up 2.3 million people each day in the world's biggest prison system? The Real Cost of Prisons Project provides the means to begin to imagine the scope, size and reach of the prison system. The unprecedented growth of the prison system over the past 30 years has been breathtaking. As large as those direct costs are, they are only a fraction of the Real Costs—the costs to children having parents taken from them, of households struggling as a wage earner is removed, of grandparents delaying retirement to raise their grandkids. These comics give us a window onto the incalculable **human** costs of mass incarceration. They also provide tools to further organizing efforts to stop it.

Over the past 30 years, the United States has increased the number of people sent to prison at a rate unmatched in this country's history.

The United States keeps people in prison at rates unheard of across the rest of the overdeveloped world. According to the International Center for Prison Studies, the U.S. incarcerates residents at almost seven times the rate that Canada sends people to prison, 5.8 times the rate of Australia, 8.6 times the rate of France and 11.9 times the rate of Japan.

The era of mass incarceration and prison building has produced activists, policy analysts, academics, artists and others whose numbers and visibility have increased over the past decade.

STATE AND FEDERAL PRISONS (1925-2005)

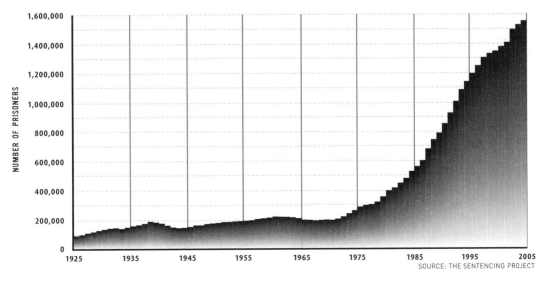

SOURCE: THE SENTENCING PROJECT

DIRECT COSTS

Add up what the 50 state systems plus the Federal prison system spend and you find the U.S. spends over $60 billion a year for prisons. Among all levels of government the U.S. spends more than $40 billion on courts and $100 billion on police.

What does $60 billion for prisons plus another $140 billion for the pipeline to put people in them buy these days? For starters, there are over 2.3 million people who work directly for the criminal justice system. One of every fifty people with jobs works for the criminal justice system, and that figure doesn't include the mushrooming private security business. About half that number work for police departments. Prisons employ about three-quarters of a million workers, and prison guards comprise the largest segment. But also employed in prisons or in the bureaucracies that build and oversee them are secretaries, warehouse workers, teachers, nurses, psychologists, planners, accountants, public relations professionals, locksmiths, doctors, human resource staff, information technology staff, gardeners and lawyers.

Most prisons don't grow their own food or generate their own electricity, water or natural gas. Most don't process their own sewage. Much of the cost of prisons is contracting for goods and services. Apart from the simple basics of food, power and water, there are more specialized needs. These include developing, marketing and insuring the bonds used to finance prison construction, running the construction firms that specialize in prison construction or sub-contracting with firms for parts of the construction bid. A few years ago we met an engineer who worked planning air conditioning and heating systems for prisons. It was a complicated job, she told us, because state rules set temperature and air quality standards for state buildings but had a different set of standards for prison cells—that is the cellblocks could get colder in the winter and hotter in the summer than office or classroom space.

At the annual American Correctional Association convention hundreds of vendors hawk the latest in equipment and services for the 21st century prison - restraint chairs, stun guns, Correctional Cable TV, and of course telephone services. Prison administrators and purchasing agents learn about how much extra can be charged for collect calls from the prisoners to their families, friends and lawyers, and how big a kickback the prison system can get from the phone companies.

Since the mid-1990s, the phrase "Prison Industrial Complex" has come to represent the physical system of prisons, courthouses, police stations, all the people who work in and for them and all the companies who sell goods or services to prisons and jails. While the exact limit of the Prison Industrial Complex may be imprecise, it must include all those whose work is essential to the prison system and those who salaries wouldn't be paid without the prison system like the TV newscasters and producers who feed us ever greater coverage of violent crime even though the violent crime rate has been falling for nearly 20 years. We would have to include politicians who attack opponents for being "soft on crime." Academics and journalists who write about crime and prisons and even paid activists who work to reform or abolish the system - no matter what their political perspective - become in odd ways in debt to prisons.

No one so far as we can tell has been able to assemble an army of bean counters big enough to really estimate what the total expenditures of that extended Prison Industrial Complex is. But it is certainly far more than the $60 billion a year the Department of Justice estimates we spend on prisons or even the $200 billion on federal, state and local law enforcement. Who knows? $500 billion? A trillion? Something approaching Iraq war costs?

THE REAL COST OF PRISONS

The Real Cost of Prisons Project is distinctly outside the mainstream. It is based on simple ideas. One is that everyone, not just people with fancy educations, can and must understand the complicated politics and economics underlying prison expansion if we are to stop that expansion. The RCPP comics demonstrate that the ideas we need to change the world can be explained simply enough and packaged attractively enough to be used by all kinds of readers from the modestly-educated to the over-educated.

Alongside the idea that prisoners and their families could understand material usually circulated only among academics and those who focus on policy is a fundamentally original notion: that however many hundreds of billions of dollars the US spends on the PIC, the **real** cost of prisons is something else again.

The hidden or indirect costs of mass incarceration are borne by the poor, a poverty tax paid disproportionately by people of color and immigrants that reaches into the pocket books of everyone who depends on government services like public education, health care or housing.

People who spend part of their lives in prison are the hardest hit and most continue to pay the rest of their lives. The "Free at Last" pages in *Prisoners of the War on Drugs* gives a quick overview of the many obstacles facing people released from prison. The formerly incarcerated have always faced discrimination especially in employment and housing. Increasingly over the past 20 years, barriers constructed originally from informal prejudice have become institutionalized legal barriers as people with felony convictions are denied employment, student aid, public housing, TANF and other services that could and should be the building blocks to help the hundreds of thousands of women and men released from prison each year to get their lives together.

Prisons are ruinous to families. The story of Denise James and her family in *Prisoners of a Hard Life* shows the sorts of pressures put on a household when one of the adults is sent to prison. Children are often sent into foster care or parceled out to members of the extended family. The loss of an income provider forces many if not most families to move. Families that can stay together face additional costs of visiting the prison, usually in distant rural locations and fees for collect calls from the

imprisoned family member, fees far greater than costs for free world collect calls. Until a successful organizing campaign stopped it, the state of New York brought in $20 million in 2002 as their cut from MCI's exclusive contract for collect calls from NY prisons, $20 million paid mostly by families of prisoners.

Because so many people in prison are taken from racially and economically segregated neighborhoods, the disproportionate financial, emotional and physical costs borne by the extended families and friends of those in prison are multiplied in the neighborhoods from which many prisoners are taken. Susan Tucker and Eric Cadora found city blocks in Brooklyn for which the state pays over $1 million per year to imprison or supervise parole for residents. They ask whether a program of "Justice Reinvestment" in which a substantial part of those funds were spent locally might provide greater public safety and opportunity.

Dina Rose and Todd Clear have discovered that neighborhoods from which too many people are taken to prison actually show smaller declines in crime than similar neighborhoods with fewer people cycling through the prison system. The impact of mass incarceration on the individual or family is multiplied when so many from a neighborhood are taken away, disrupting the local economy and the sorts of informal social controls (like people knowing each other) that prevent crime in the first place. The burden on the neighborhood is more than the sum of the burden on the individuals in it.

Over the past decade there has been an abundance of books, documentary films and videos, articles and conferences about the prison system. The RCPP comics and the rest of The Real Cost of Prisons Project differ from most of those materials in their political vision. By making the politics and economics of prisons accessible to a wide readership and providing an expansive vision of the costs of mass incarceration, the RCPP has provided important tools to dismantle the system.

These comic books provide a uniquely accurate description of the prison system. Their brilliance lies in their originality and adaptability. In beginning to explain all the costs that so many of us are paying to keep 2.3 million people in U.S. prisons, the RCPP offers multiple points of vulnerability of that system and thereby multiple locations from which to work against it.

PRISON TOWN ORGANIZING

The process of finding a place to put a prison has never been easy, but during the prison building boom of the 1980s and 90s, departments of correction found that rural towns, devastated by the farm crisis and related economic woes, were receptive to hearing about "recession-proof" industries with multi-million dollar payrolls. Who wouldn't want hundreds of new state employees to prop up a sagging economy? As it turned out the economic promise of hosting a prison didn't pay off for the overwhelming majority of prison towns, as you can see in the *Prison Town: Paying the Price* comic book.

In reality, many towns that took prisons were worse off having done it than similar towns that didn't. The real cost paid by prison towns became a principle around which people in towns targeted for new prisons could organize. In town after town across the country, a few hard-headed residents would buttonhole neighbors, speak at PTA and club meetings and churches, and editorialize at the local diner to educate the town as to the real cost of "hosting" a prison in order to mobilize public opinion against the proposed prison and pressure the city council to kill the project.

THE REAL COST TO SCHOOLS

In his book *Newjack: Guarding Sing Sing*, Ted Conover recounts a conversation he had with a long time prisoner named Larson. Conover is surprised to find that Larson, imprisoned in the ancient and decrepit Sing Sing, opposes plans the state of New York has to build new prisons. Larson explains:

"Anyone planning a prison they're not going to build for ten or fifteen years is planning for a child, planning prison for somebody who's a child right now. So you see? They've already given up on that child! They already expect that child to fail. Now why, if you could keep that from happening, if you could send that child to a good school and help his family stay together - if you could do that, why are you spending that money to put him in jail?"

As Larson understands, what the state spends money building creates a political, economic and cultural inertia. If you're building prisons now, you expect to hire more police to arrest more kids next year. If you build schools now, you expect to hire more teachers next year to better educate kids.

Probably the most famous of the education not incarceration campaigns was the long fight to close Tallulah youth prison in northeast Louisiana. Tallulah was scandal-ridden from the moment the first young prisoners arrived for both the extraordinary levels of violence inside and the corrupt relationship between its private operators and the state of Louisiana. Neither brutality nor corruption is unusual, but at Tallulah, the levels were off the charts. Organizing through the Juvenile Justice Project and Families and Friends of Louisiana's Incarcerated Children, parents, youth and other activists closed Tallulah.

In response, the state planned to reopen the youth prison as an adult prison, but local residents had lived in the shadow of a prison long enough and demanded that the state turn the prison into an educational facility in which the youth and adults of the region could learn marketable skills.

"GENDER-RESPONSIVE PRISONS"

For decades, advocates for women in prison have used arguments about the horrors inflicted on women in prison to push for changes in prison policies and/or a reduction in women in prison. Recently, activists and advocates in California have fought over whether the state should expand its prison system with a series of "gender-responsive" Female Reentry Community Corrections Centers, or women's mini-prisons as they are usually called.

The conflict between the two camps of activists and advocates was about how the real costs of prison on women and their children are better addressed: by working to free the prison system of its gender biases (retraining staff, new policies, "gender-responsive" programming and "gender-responsive" design of the prisons) or by working to free numbers of women in prison and returning them (and resources to help in their transition) to their children and other loved ones.

For women whose addiction has been criminalized, therefore landing them in jail or prison instead of drug treatment, "gender-responsive treatment" while controlled by a prison is impossible. Gender-responsive treatment for women requires support in nurturing a strong sense of self, achieving health holistically and moving towards empowerment. Addiction constricts a woman's life. So does incarceration.

In Western Massachusetts, a new jail was recently built for women. To justify this $26 million regional facility, the jail's assistant superintendent was quoted in a local newspaper as saying "We incarcerate to set free." The perversity of this comment lies in its attempt to convince the public that locking more women in jail will reduce the social costs to the incarcerated women, their children and other loved ones and the broader community.

CONCLUSION

The Real Cost of Prisons comics provide us with a great resource for making connections between issues and among groups toiling in the often separated worlds of political organizing. They are bridges to those fighting racism, homelessness and police brutality and to those working on immigrants' rights, health care, living wages, LGBT rights, women's issues, education, environmental justice and many other issues. While three comics don't

lay out every detail needed to make all the necessary connections, they show that everyone can build links using simple ideas: What is the real cost of prison expansion to immigrants in our major cities? What is the real cost of the high drop-out (or push-out) rate in our schools and the common "zero tolerance" policies that push kids into the "School-to-Prison Pipeline"?

A crucial challenge facing those who would stop the damage inflicted by the prison system is to understand how prisons hurt particular types of people and how to tie the issues that a variety of people are concerned about today to a deeper understanding of the prison system. The great value of The Real Cost of Prisons has been to show us how the system of mass incarceration permeates our lives, who is paying the costs of that system and the many ways the system is vulnerable to people who put their thought and effort into organizing to shrink it.

Thanks to Lois Ahrens, Ellen Miller-Mack and Marc Mauer.

Ruth Wilson Gilmore is the author of Golden Gulag and a member of Critical Resistance and the California Prison Moratorium Project. Craig Gilmore is an organizer with California Prison Moratorium Project and CURB.

the real cost of prisons project™

Prison Town

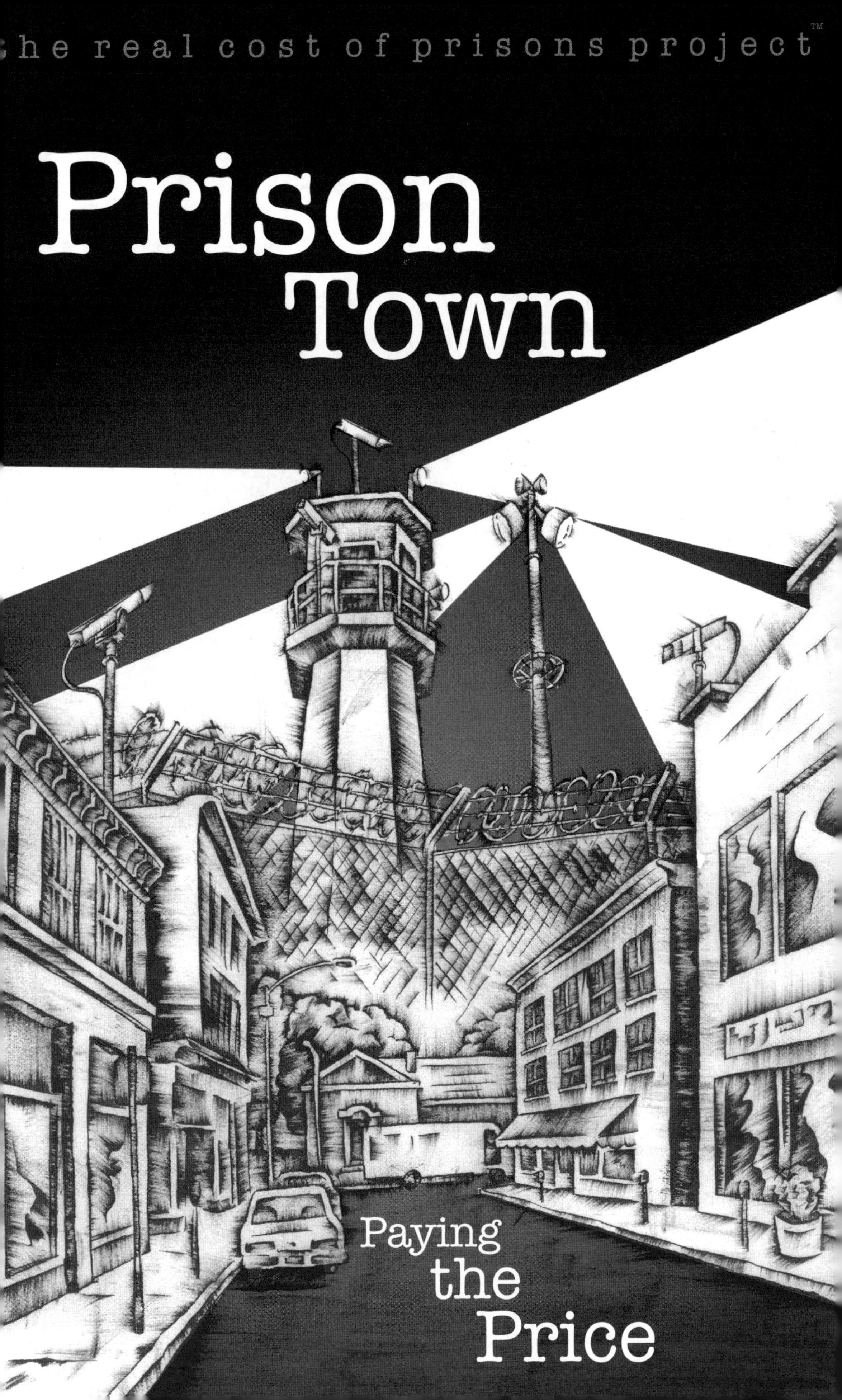

Paying the Price

the real cost of prisons project

www.realcostofprisons.org • info@realcostofprisons.org

Prison Town
Paying the Price

Artist: Kevin Pyle • Writers: Kevin Pyle & Craig Gilmore

Real Cost of Financing and Siting of Prisons writer/presenter: Craig Gilmore

Art Director & Cover Design: Chris Shadoian

Real Cost of Prisons Project Director: Lois Ahrens

The Real Cost of Prisons Project brings together prison/justice policy activists with political economists to create workshops and materials which explore both the immediate and long-term costs of mass incarceration on the individual, her/his family, community and the nation.

Two additional comic books are part of this series: *Prisoners of the War on Drugs* and *Prisoners of Hard Times: Women and Children.* If you would like copies of these comic books to assist your group in its organizing work, contact Lois Ahrens. Or you can go to www.realcostofprisons.org and download the entire series.

The Real Cost of Prisons Project is an activity of The Sentencing Project, a Washington, DC based non-profit dedicated to reducing over-reliance on incarceration. The Real Cost of Prisons Project is supported by a grant from the Community Advocacy Project of the Open Society Institute.

THANK YOU

Ruth Wilson Gilmore, Tracy Huling, Peter Wagner, Eric Cadora, Todd Clear, Dina Rose, N.C. Christopher Couch, James Heinz, Marc Mauer, Malcolm Young, Raquiba LaBrie, William Johnston and Helena Huang.

ISBN: 0-9763856-0-0 • Art and stories are © and TM 2005 The Real Cost of Prisons Project. All Rights Reserved. Write to us at 5 Warfield Place, Northampton, MA 01060. Printed in Canada.

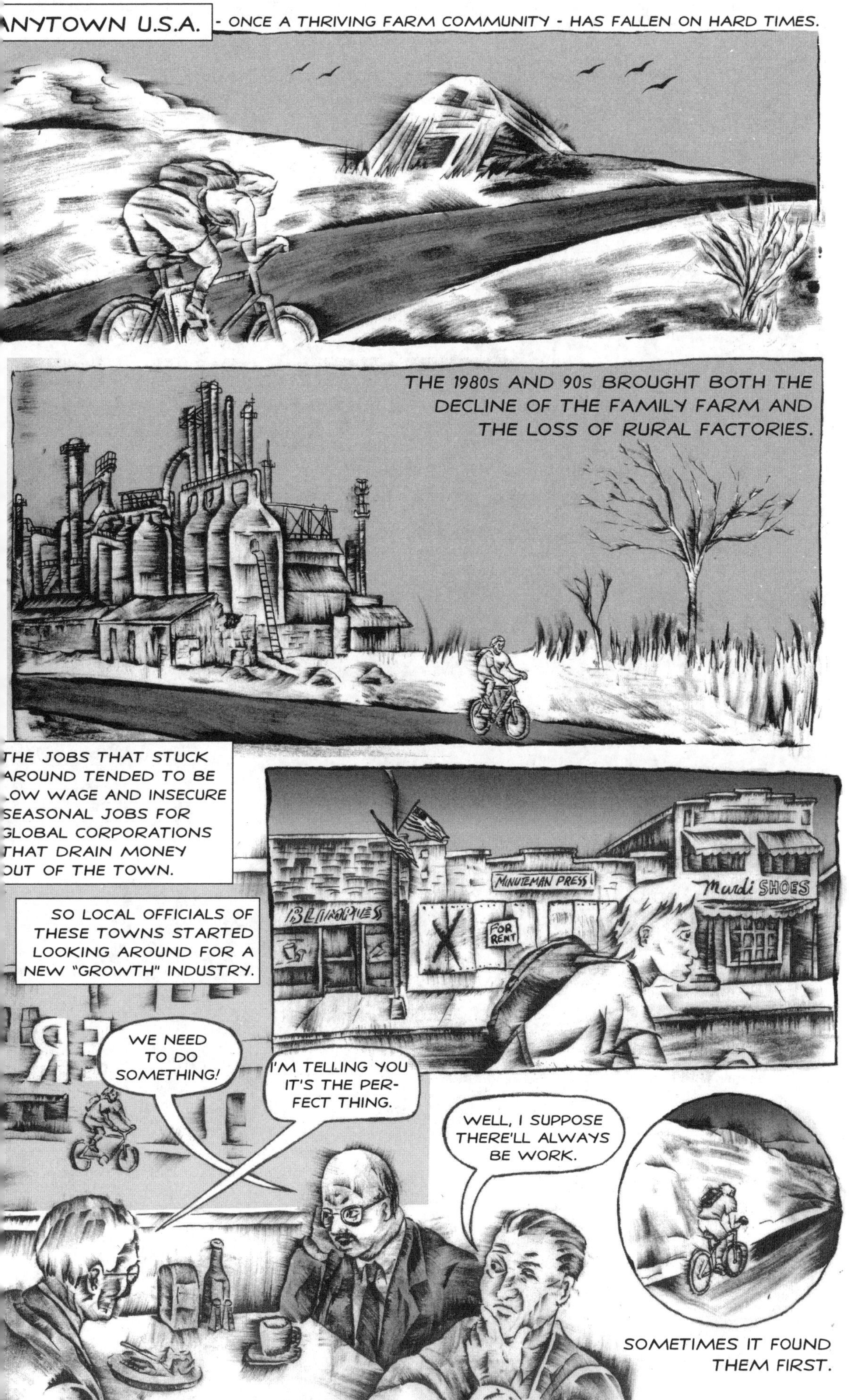
ANYTOWN U.S.A. - ONCE A THRIVING FARM COMMUNITY - HAS FALLEN ON HARD TIMES.
THE 1980s AND 90s BROUGHT BOTH THE DECLINE OF THE FAMILY FARM AND THE LOSS OF RURAL FACTORIES.
THE JOBS THAT STUCK AROUND TENDED TO BE LOW WAGE AND INSECURE SEASONAL JOBS FOR GLOBAL CORPORATIONS THAT DRAIN MONEY OUT OF THE TOWN.
MINUTEMAN PRESS
FOR RENT
Mardi SHOES
SO LOCAL OFFICIALS OF THESE TOWNS STARTED LOOKING AROUND FOR A NEW "GROWTH" INDUSTRY.
WE NEED TO DO SOMETHING!
I'M TELLING YOU IT'S THE PER-FECT THING.
WELL, I SUPPOSE THERE'LL ALWAYS BE WORK.
SOMETIMES IT FOUND THEM FIRST.

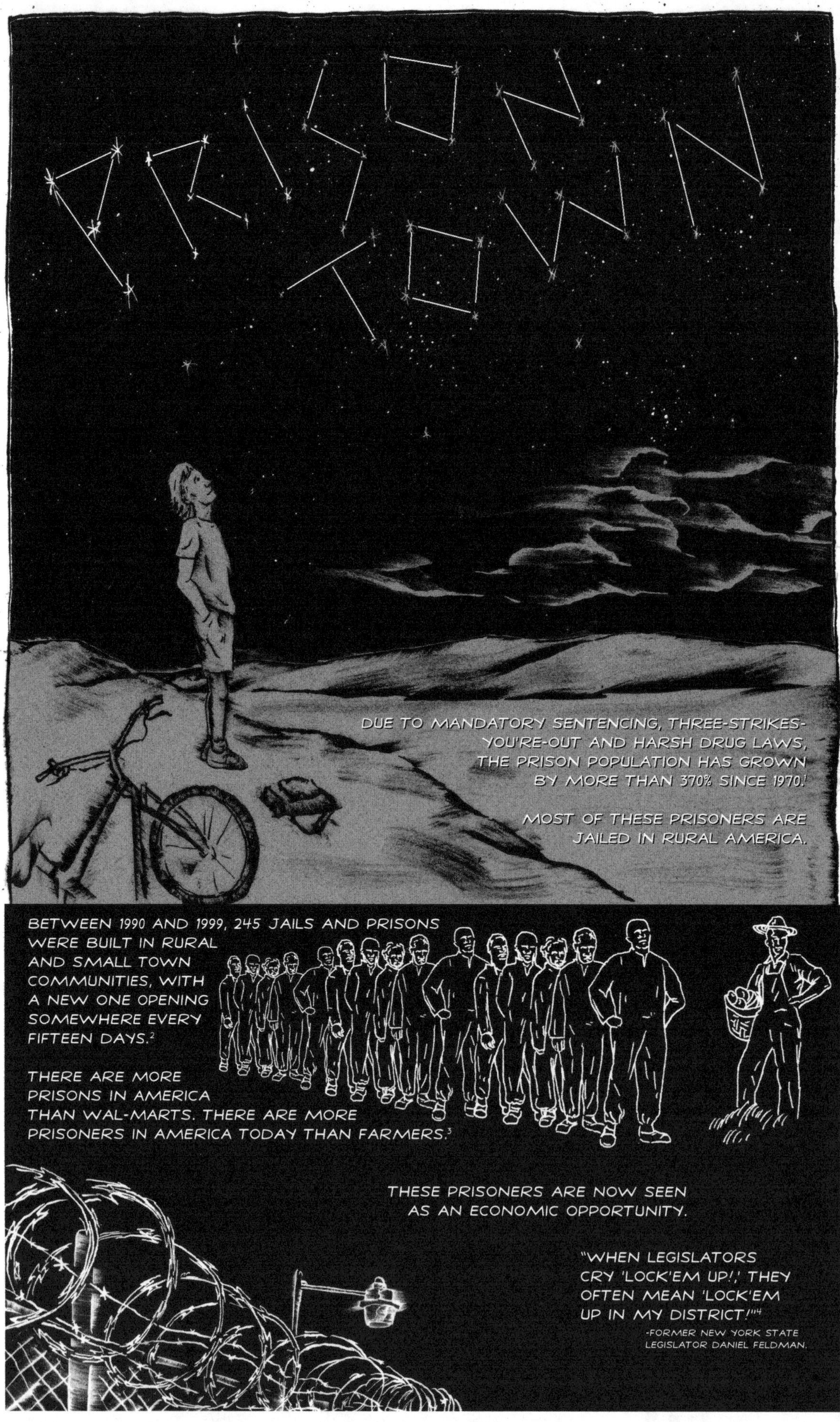
PRISON TOWN
DUE TO MANDATORY SENTENCING, THREE-STRIKES-YOU'RE-OUT AND HARSH DRUG LAWS, THE PRISON POPULATION HAS GROWN BY MORE THAN 370% SINCE 1970.[1]
MOST OF THESE PRISONERS ARE JAILED IN RURAL AMERICA.
BETWEEN 1990 AND 1999, 245 JAILS AND PRISONS WERE BUILT IN RURAL AND SMALL TOWN COMMUNITIES, WITH A NEW ONE OPENING SOMEWHERE EVERY FIFTEEN DAYS.[2]
THERE ARE MORE PRISONS IN AMERICA THAN WAL-MARTS. THERE ARE MORE PRISONERS IN AMERICA TODAY THAN FARMERS.[3]
THESE PRISONERS ARE NOW SEEN AS AN ECONOMIC OPPORTUNITY.
"WHEN LEGISLATORS CRY 'LOCK'EM UP!,' THEY OFTEN MEAN 'LOCK'EM UP IN MY DISTRICT!'"[4]
-FORMER NEW YORK STATE LEGISLATOR DANIEL FELDMAN.

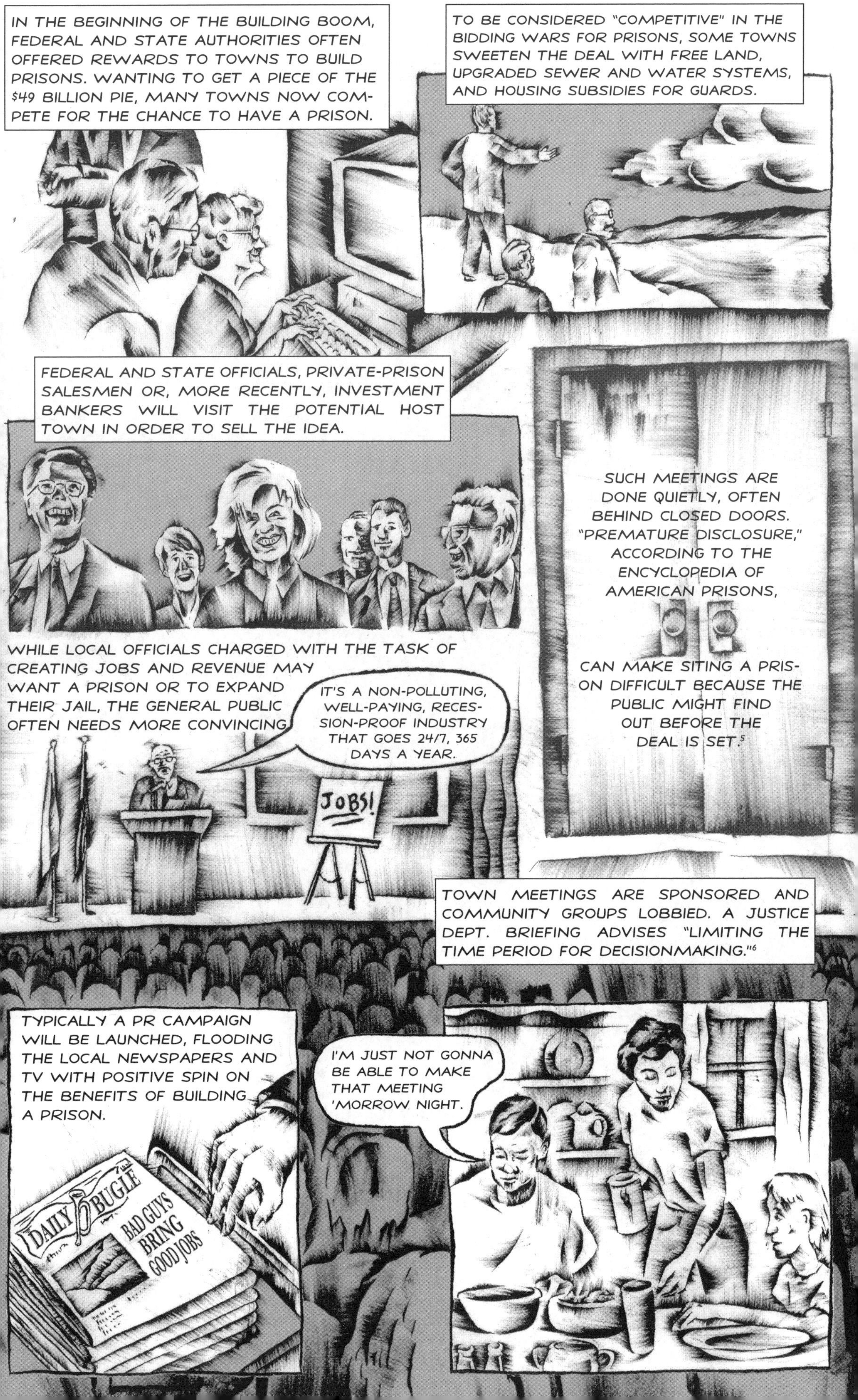
IN THE BEGINNING OF THE BUILDING BOOM, FEDERAL AND STATE AUTHORITIES OFTEN OFFERED REWARDS TO TOWNS TO BUILD PRISONS. WANTING TO GET A PIECE OF THE $49 BILLION PIE, MANY TOWNS NOW COMPETE FOR THE CHANCE TO HAVE A PRISON.
TO BE CONSIDERED "COMPETITIVE" IN THE BIDDING WARS FOR PRISONS, SOME TOWNS SWEETEN THE DEAL WITH FREE LAND, UPGRADED SEWER AND WATER SYSTEMS, AND HOUSING SUBSIDIES FOR GUARDS.
FEDERAL AND STATE OFFICIALS, PRIVATE-PRISON SALESMEN OR, MORE RECENTLY, INVESTMENT BANKERS WILL VISIT THE POTENTIAL HOST TOWN IN ORDER TO SELL THE IDEA.
SUCH MEETINGS ARE DONE QUIETLY, OFTEN BEHIND CLOSED DOORS. "PREMATURE DISCLOSURE," ACCORDING TO THE ENCYCLOPEDIA OF AMERICAN PRISONS,
CAN MAKE SITING A PRISON DIFFICULT BECAUSE THE PUBLIC MIGHT FIND OUT BEFORE THE DEAL IS SET.[5]
WHILE LOCAL OFFICIALS CHARGED WITH THE TASK OF CREATING JOBS AND REVENUE MAY WANT A PRISON OR TO EXPAND THEIR JAIL, THE GENERAL PUBLIC OFTEN NEEDS MORE CONVINCING.
IT'S A NON-POLLUTING, WELL-PAYING, RECESSION-PROOF INDUSTRY THAT GOES 24/7, 365 DAYS A YEAR.
JOBS!
TOWN MEETINGS ARE SPONSORED AND COMMUNITY GROUPS LOBBIED. A JUSTICE DEPT. BRIEFING ADVISES "LIMITING THE TIME PERIOD FOR DECISIONMAKING."[6]
TYPICALLY A PR CAMPAIGN WILL BE LAUNCHED, FLOODING THE LOCAL NEWSPAPERS AND TV WITH POSITIVE SPIN ON THE BENEFITS OF BUILDING A PRISON.
DAILY BUGLE
BAD GUYS BRING GOOD JOBS
I'M JUST NOT GONNA BE ABLE TO MAKE THAT MEETING 'MORROW NIGHT.

IN 1996, OREGON SITED SIX PRISONS IN SIX MONTHS UNDER OREGON'S "SUPER SITING LAW" WHICH MADE PRISONS EXEMPT FROM STATE LEVEL ENVIRONMENTAL REVIEW.[7]

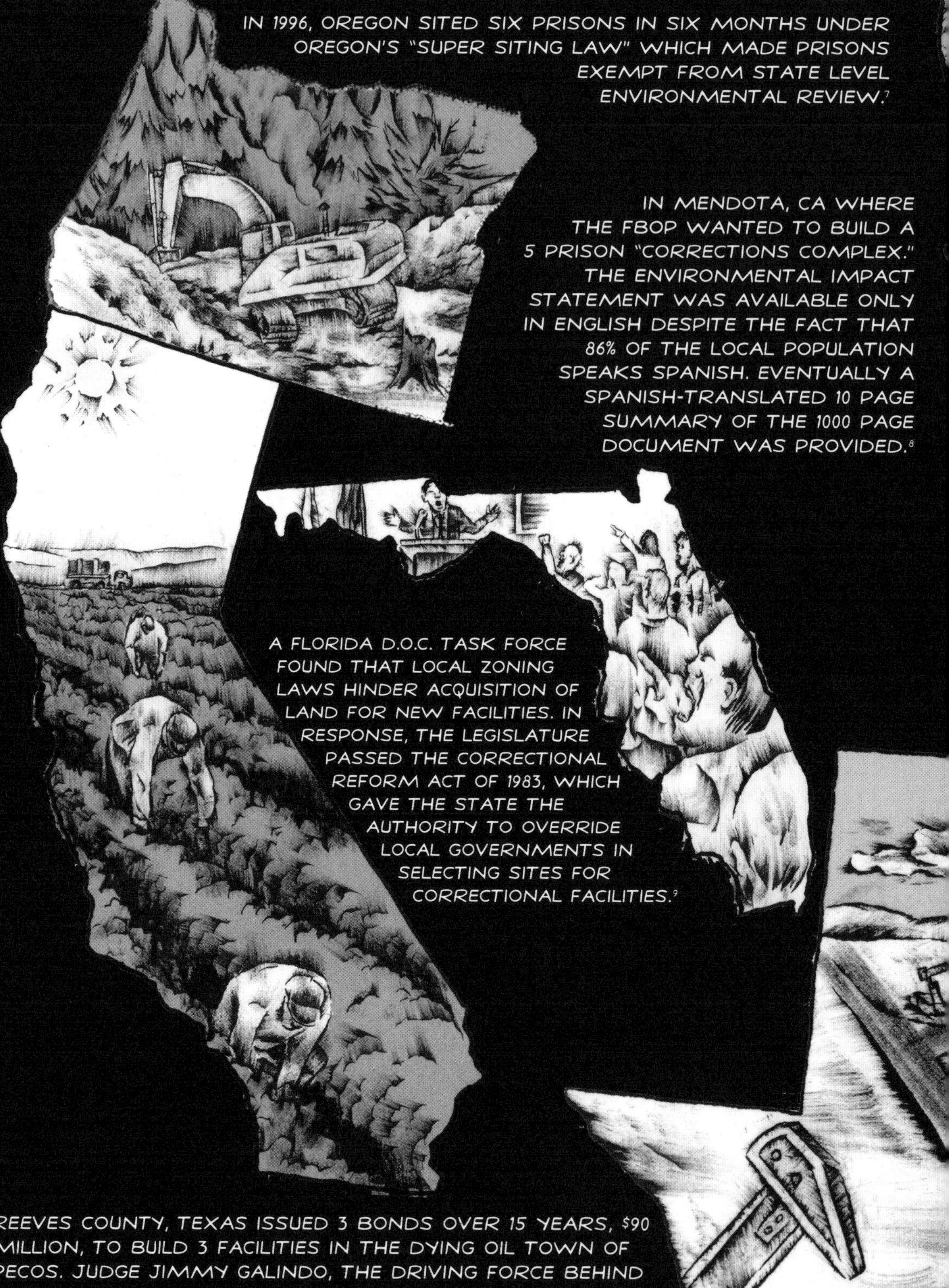

IN MENDOTA, CA WHERE THE FBOP WANTED TO BUILD A 5 PRISON "CORRECTIONS COMPLEX." THE ENVIRONMENTAL IMPACT STATEMENT WAS AVAILABLE ONLY IN ENGLISH DESPITE THE FACT THAT 86% OF THE LOCAL POPULATION SPEAKS SPANISH. EVENTUALLY A SPANISH-TRANSLATED 10 PAGE SUMMARY OF THE 1000 PAGE DOCUMENT WAS PROVIDED.[8]

A FLORIDA D.O.C. TASK FORCE FOUND THAT LOCAL ZONING LAWS HINDER ACQUISITION OF LAND FOR NEW FACILITIES. IN RESPONSE, THE LEGISLATURE PASSED THE CORRECTIONAL REFORM ACT OF 1983, WHICH GAVE THE STATE THE AUTHORITY TO OVERRIDE LOCAL GOVERNMENTS IN SELECTING SITES FOR CORRECTIONAL FACILITIES.[9]

REEVES COUNTY, TEXAS ISSUED 3 BONDS OVER 15 YEARS, $90 MILLION, TO BUILD 3 FACILITIES IN THE DYING OIL TOWN OF PECOS. JUDGE JIMMY GALINDO, THE DRIVING FORCE BEHIND THE DEAL SAYS: ". . . WE LIVE IN A PART OF THE COUNTRY WHERE IT'S VERY DIFFICULT TO CREATE AND SUSTAIN JOBS IN A GLOBAL MARKET. [PRISONS] BECOME A VERY CLEAN INDUSTRY FOR US TO PROVIDE EMPLOYMENT TO CITIZENS."
"I LOOK AT IT AS A COMMUNITY DEVELOPMENT PROJECT."[10]

MANY MUNICIPALITIES ARE EXPANDING THEIR JAIL FACILITIES IN ORDER TO RENT BEDS TO OVERCROWDED FEDERAL AND STATE PRISONS.

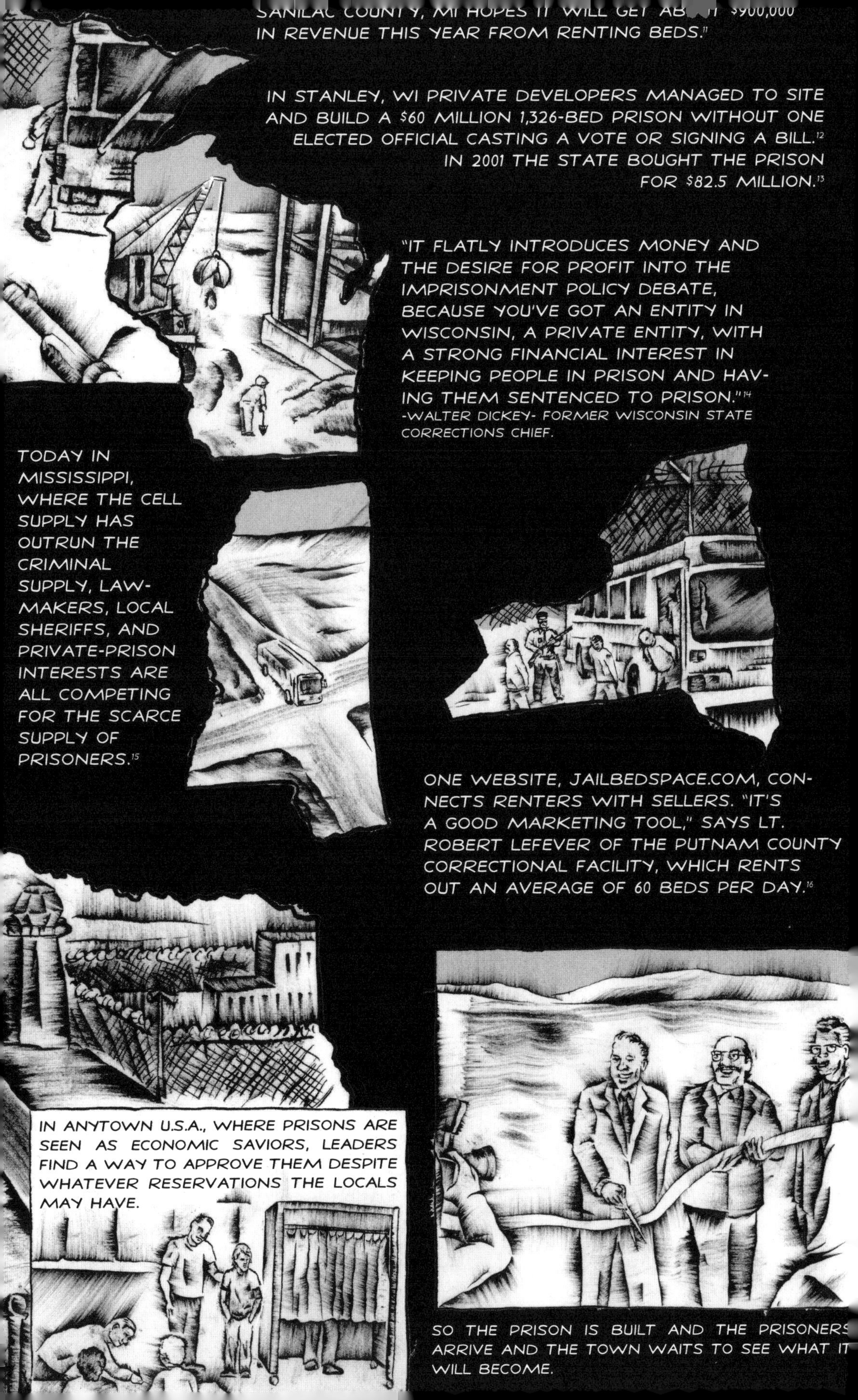
SANILAC COUNTY, MI HOPES IT WILL GET AB T $900,000 IN REVENUE THIS YEAR FROM RENTING BEDS."
IN STANLEY, WI PRIVATE DEVELOPERS MANAGED TO SITE AND BUILD A $60 MILLION 1,326-BED PRISON WITHOUT ONE ELECTED OFFICIAL CASTING A VOTE OR SIGNING A BILL.[12] IN 2001 THE STATE BOUGHT THE PRISON FOR $82.5 MILLION.[13]
"IT FLATLY INTRODUCES MONEY AND THE DESIRE FOR PROFIT INTO THE IMPRISONMENT POLICY DEBATE, BECAUSE YOU'VE GOT AN ENTITY IN WISCONSIN, A PRIVATE ENTITY, WITH A STRONG FINANCIAL INTEREST IN KEEPING PEOPLE IN PRISON AND HAVING THEM SENTENCED TO PRISON."[14]
-WALTER DICKEY- FORMER WISCONSIN STATE CORRECTIONS CHIEF.
TODAY IN MISSISSIPPI, WHERE THE CELL SUPPLY HAS OUTRUN THE CRIMINAL SUPPLY, LAWMAKERS, LOCAL SHERIFFS, AND PRIVATE-PRISON INTERESTS ARE ALL COMPETING FOR THE SCARCE SUPPLY OF PRISONERS.[15]
ONE WEBSITE, JAILBEDSPACE.COM, CONNECTS RENTERS WITH SELLERS. "IT'S A GOOD MARKETING TOOL," SAYS LT. ROBERT LEFEVER OF THE PUTNAM COUNTY CORRECTIONAL FACILITY, WHICH RENTS OUT AN AVERAGE OF 60 BEDS PER DAY.[16]
IN ANYTOWN U.S.A., WHERE PRISONS ARE SEEN AS ECONOMIC SAVIORS, LEADERS FIND A WAY TO APPROVE THEM DESPITE WHATEVER RESERVATIONS THE LOCALS MAY HAVE.
SO THE PRISON IS BUILT AND THE PRISONERS ARRIVE AND THE TOWN WAITS TO SEE WHAT IT WILL BECOME.

How Prisons Are Paid For (and who really pays?)

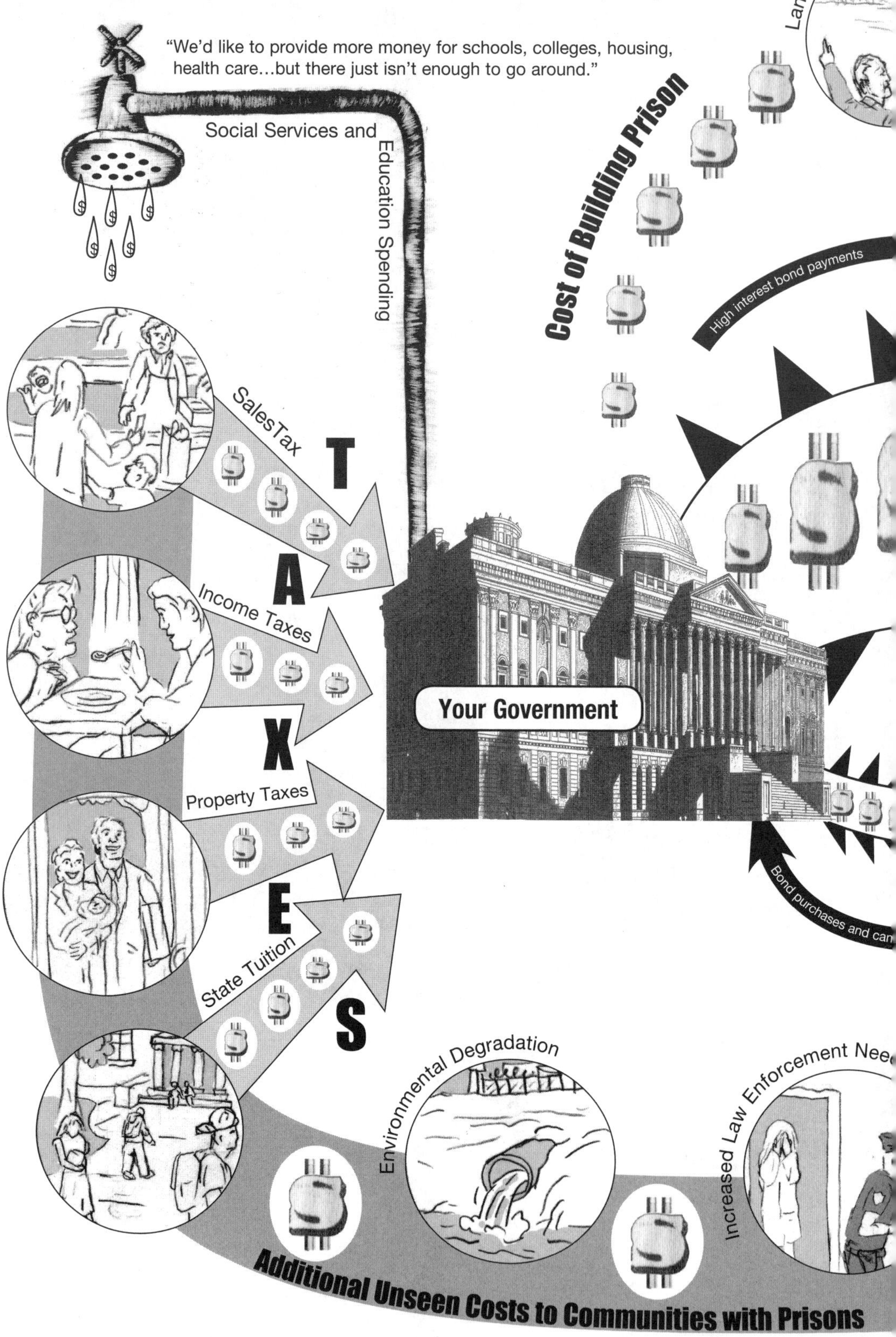
"We'd like to provide more money for schools, colleges, housing, health care...but there just isn't enough to go around."
Social Services and Education Spending
Cost of Building Prison
Land costs
High interest bond payments
SalesTax
Income Taxes
Property Taxes
State Tuition
TAXES
Your Government
Bond purchases and can
Environmental Degradation
Increased Law Enforcement Nee
Additional Unseen Costs to Communities with Prisons

What is a bond? A bond is a loan made to a government. Governments pay investment bankers to make the loan attractive ('structure the deal') and find lenders ('issue the bonds'). Governments then pay lenders ('bondholders') principal and interest on the loans.

Governments issue two broad categories of bond: General Obligation (GO) bonds and Revenue Bonds. General Obligation bonds are guaranteed by the taxing power of the state. Most GO Bonds require approval by the voters, and in many states by 2/3 of the voters. Revenue Bonds are designed to be paid off by revenues generated by the project being built, like highway tolls, bridge tolls, student tuition, etc.

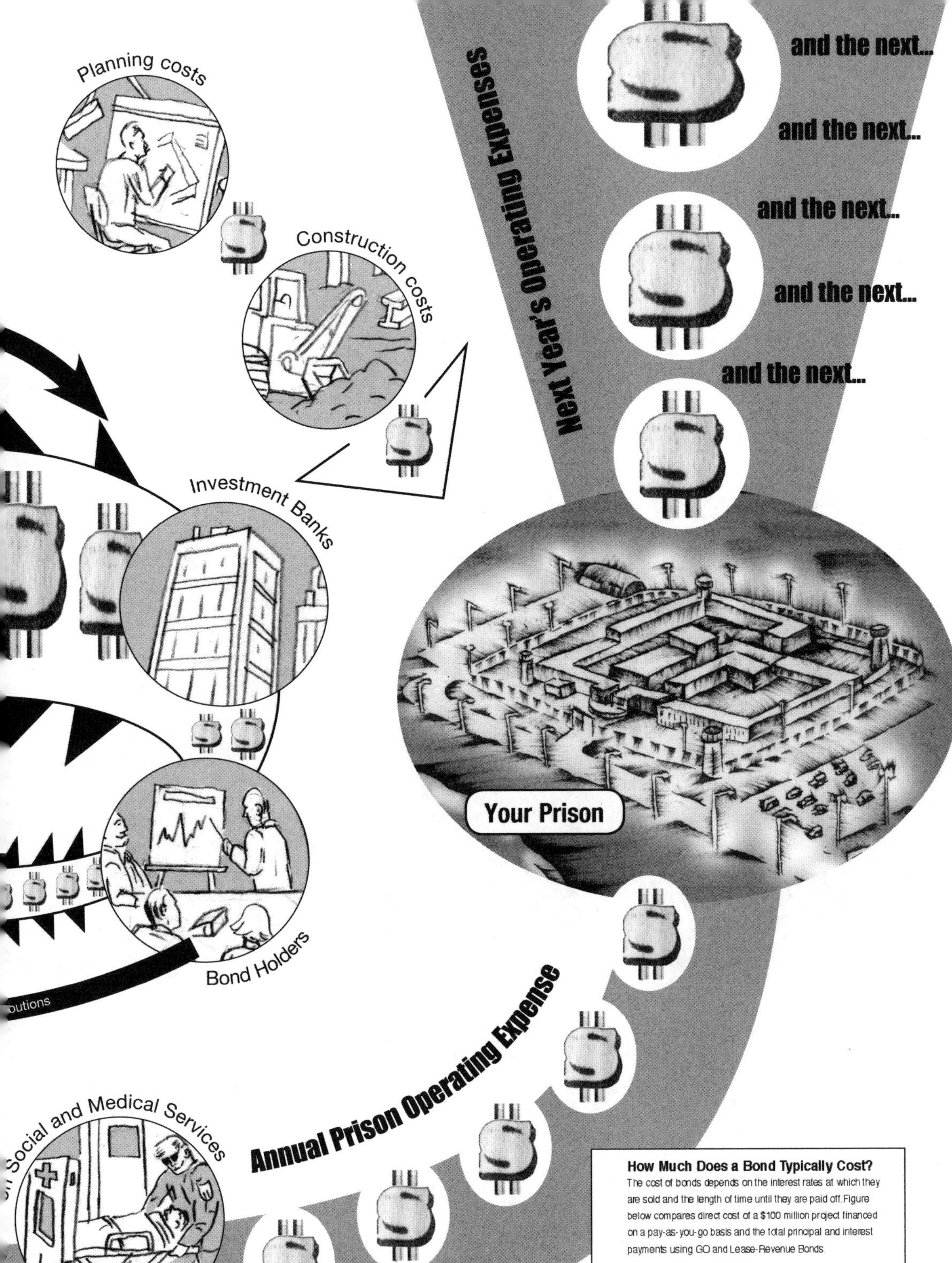
Planning costs
Construction costs
Investment Banks
Bond Holders
butions
Social and Medical Services
Next Year's Operating Expenses
and the next...
and the next...
and the next...
and the next...
and the next...
Your Prison
Annual Prison Operating Expense

How Much Does a Bond Typically Cost?

The cost of bonds depends on the interest rates at which they are sold and the length of time until they are paid off. Figure below compares direct cost of a $100 million project financed on a pay-as-you-go basis and the total principal and interest payments using GO and Lease-Revenue Bonds.

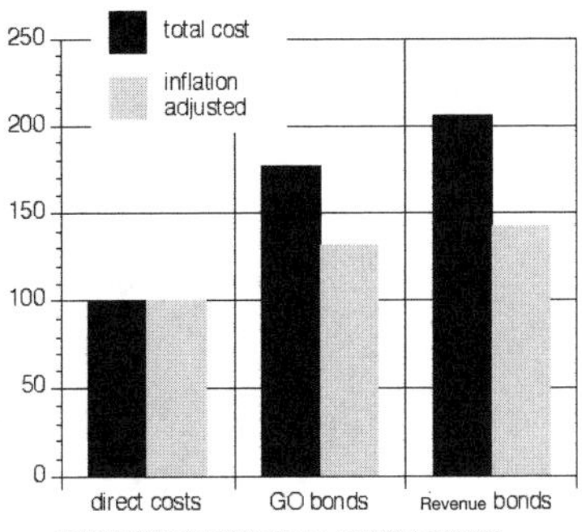
250
200
150
100
50
0
total cost
inflation adjusted
direct costs
GO bonds
Revenue bonds

source: A Primer on State Bonds. Jan.1998. Legislative Analyst's Office, California. available at: http://www.lao.ca.gov

Most prisons are now built with some form of Revenue Bond, even though prisons generate no real revenue and Revenue Bonds cost taxpayers more to repay. Why would a state use the most expensive way to borrow money to build prisons? Because voters have consistently voted down GO Bonds to build more prisons. Using revenue bonds to build prisons is a means of getting around the voters and taxpayers.

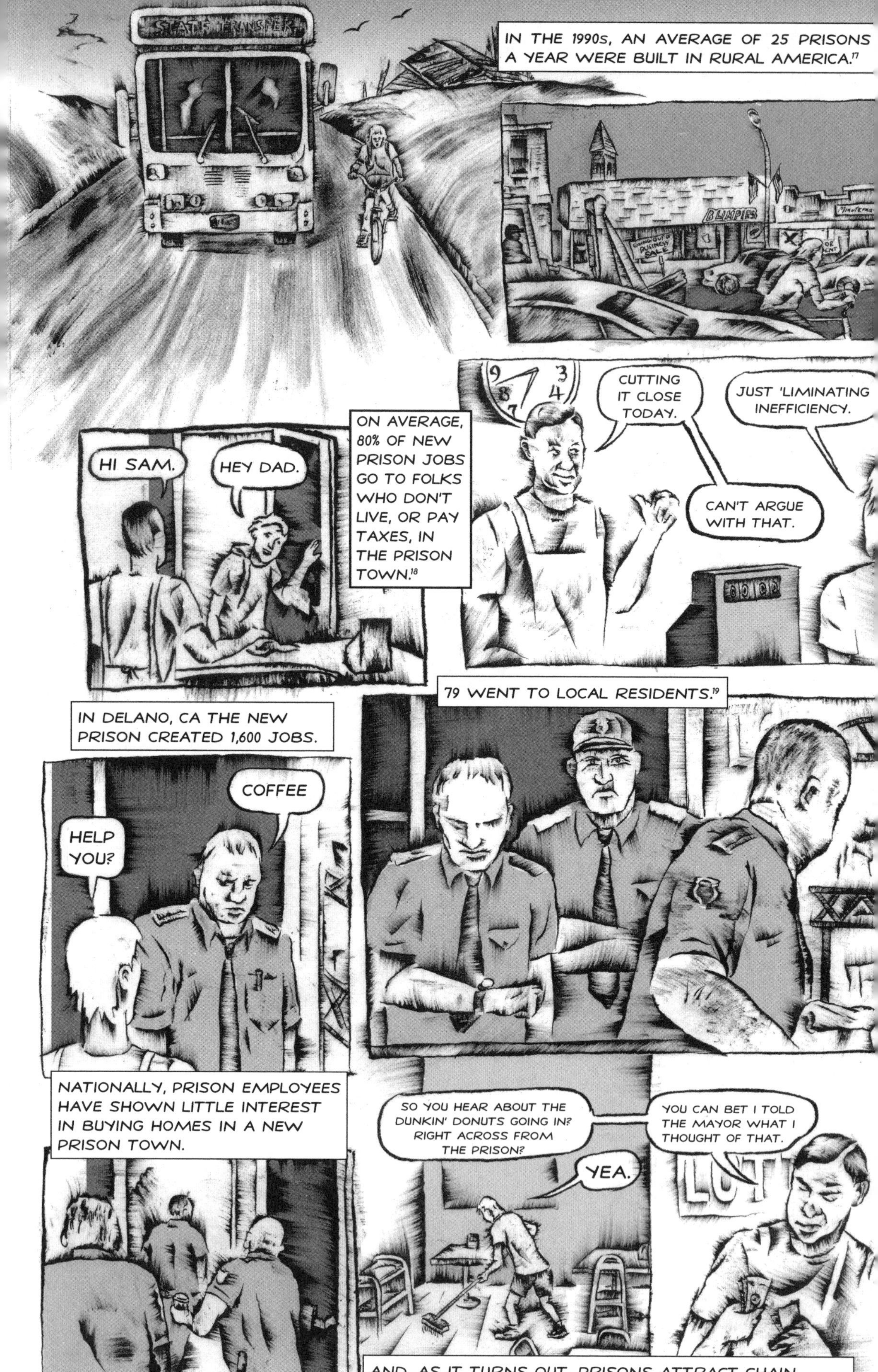
STATE TRANSFER
IN THE 1990S, AN AVERAGE OF 25 PRISONS A YEAR WERE BUILT IN RURAL AMERICA.[17]
BLIMPIES
HI SAM.
HEY DAD.
ON AVERAGE, 80% OF NEW PRISON JOBS GO TO FOLKS WHO DON'T LIVE, OR PAY TAXES, IN THE PRISON TOWN.[18]
CUTTING IT CLOSE TODAY.
JUST 'LIMINATING INEFFICIENCY.
CAN'T ARGUE WITH THAT.
IN DELANO, CA THE NEW PRISON CREATED 1,600 JOBS.
79 WENT TO LOCAL RESIDENTS.[19]
COFFEE
HELP YOU?
NATIONALLY, PRISON EMPLOYEES HAVE SHOWN LITTLE INTEREST IN BUYING HOMES IN A NEW PRISON TOWN.
SO YOU HEAR ABOUT THE DUNKIN' DONUTS GOING IN? RIGHT ACROSS FROM THE PRISON?
YOU CAN BET I TOLD THE MAYOR WHAT I THOUGHT OF THAT.
YEA.
AND, AS IT TURNS OUT, PRISONS ATTRACT CHAIN STORES, WHICH PUSH OUT LOCALLY-OWNED BUSINESS.[20]

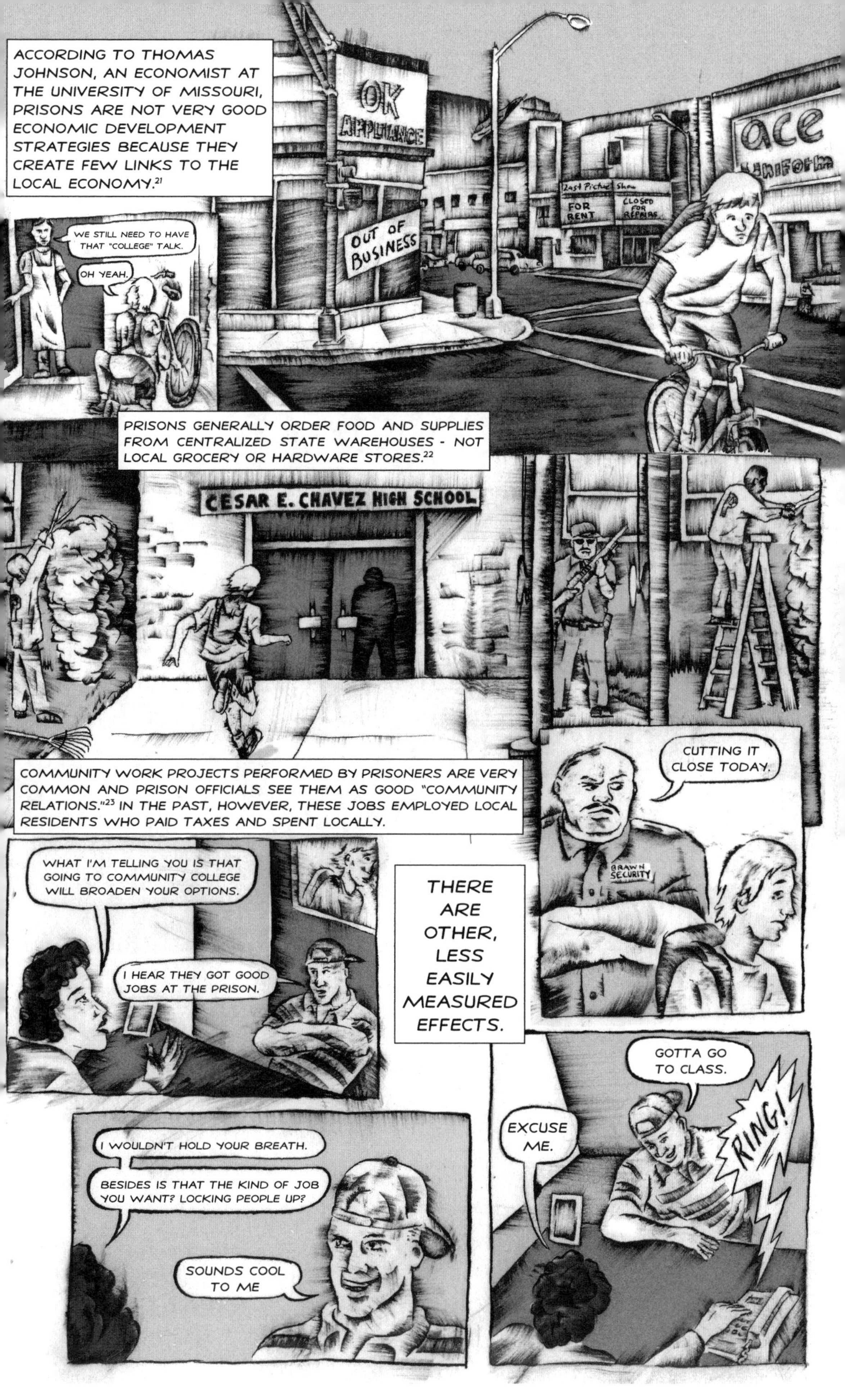
ACCORDING TO THOMAS JOHNSON, AN ECONOMIST AT THE UNIVERSITY OF MISSOURI, PRISONS ARE NOT VERY GOOD ECONOMIC DEVELOPMENT STRATEGIES BECAUSE THEY CREATE FEW LINKS TO THE LOCAL ECONOMY.[21]
OK APPLIANCE
ace Uniform
Last Picture Show
FOR RENT
CLOSED FOR REPAIRS
OUT OF BUSINESS
WE STILL NEED TO HAVE THAT "COLLEGE" TALK.
OH YEAH.
PRISONS GENERALLY ORDER FOOD AND SUPPLIES FROM CENTRALIZED STATE WAREHOUSES - NOT LOCAL GROCERY OR HARDWARE STORES.[22]
CESAR E. CHAVEZ HIGH SCHOOL
COMMUNITY WORK PROJECTS PERFORMED BY PRISONERS ARE VERY COMMON AND PRISON OFFICIALS SEE THEM AS GOOD "COMMUNITY RELATIONS."[23] IN THE PAST, HOWEVER, THESE JOBS EMPLOYED LOCAL RESIDENTS WHO PAID TAXES AND SPENT LOCALLY.
CUTTING IT CLOSE TODAY.
BRAWN SECURITY
WHAT I'M TELLING YOU IS THAT GOING TO COMMUNITY COLLEGE WILL BROADEN YOUR OPTIONS.
I HEAR THEY GOT GOOD JOBS AT THE PRISON.
THERE ARE OTHER, LESS EASILY MEASURED EFFECTS.
I WOULDN'T HOLD YOUR BREATH.
BESIDES IS THAT THE KIND OF JOB YOU WANT? LOCKING PEOPLE UP?
SOUNDS COOL TO ME
GOTTA GO TO CLASS.
EXCUSE ME.
RING!

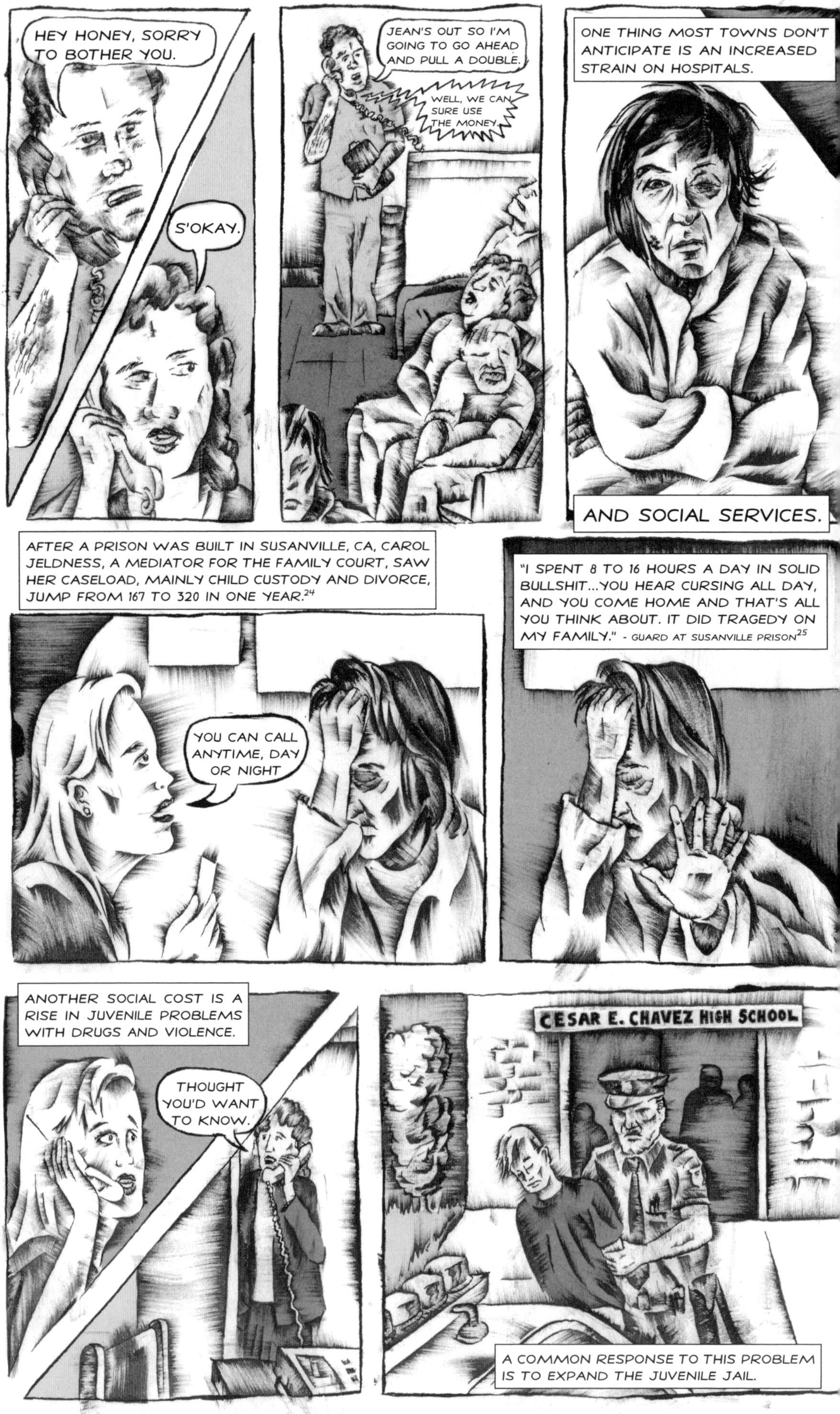
HEY HONEY, SORRY TO BOTHER YOU.
S'OKAY.
JEAN'S OUT SO I'M GOING TO GO AHEAD AND PULL A DOUBLE.
WELL, WE CAN SURE USE THE MONEY.
ONE THING MOST TOWNS DON'T ANTICIPATE IS AN INCREASED STRAIN ON HOSPITALS.
AND SOCIAL SERVICES.
AFTER A PRISON WAS BUILT IN SUSANVILLE, CA, CAROL JELDNESS, A MEDIATOR FOR THE FAMILY COURT, SAW HER CASELOAD, MAINLY CHILD CUSTODY AND DIVORCE, JUMP FROM 167 TO 320 IN ONE YEAR.[24]
YOU CAN CALL ANYTIME, DAY OR NIGHT
"I SPENT 8 TO 16 HOURS A DAY IN SOLID BULLSHIT...YOU HEAR CURSING ALL DAY, AND YOU COME HOME AND THAT'S ALL YOU THINK ABOUT. IT DID TRAGEDY ON MY FAMILY." - GUARD AT SUSANVILLE PRISON[25]
ANOTHER SOCIAL COST IS A RISE IN JUVENILE PROBLEMS WITH DRUGS AND VIOLENCE.
THOUGHT YOU'D WANT TO KNOW.
CESAR E. CHAVEZ HIGH SCHOOL
A COMMON RESPONSE TO THIS PROBLEM IS TO EXPAND THE JUVENILE JAIL.

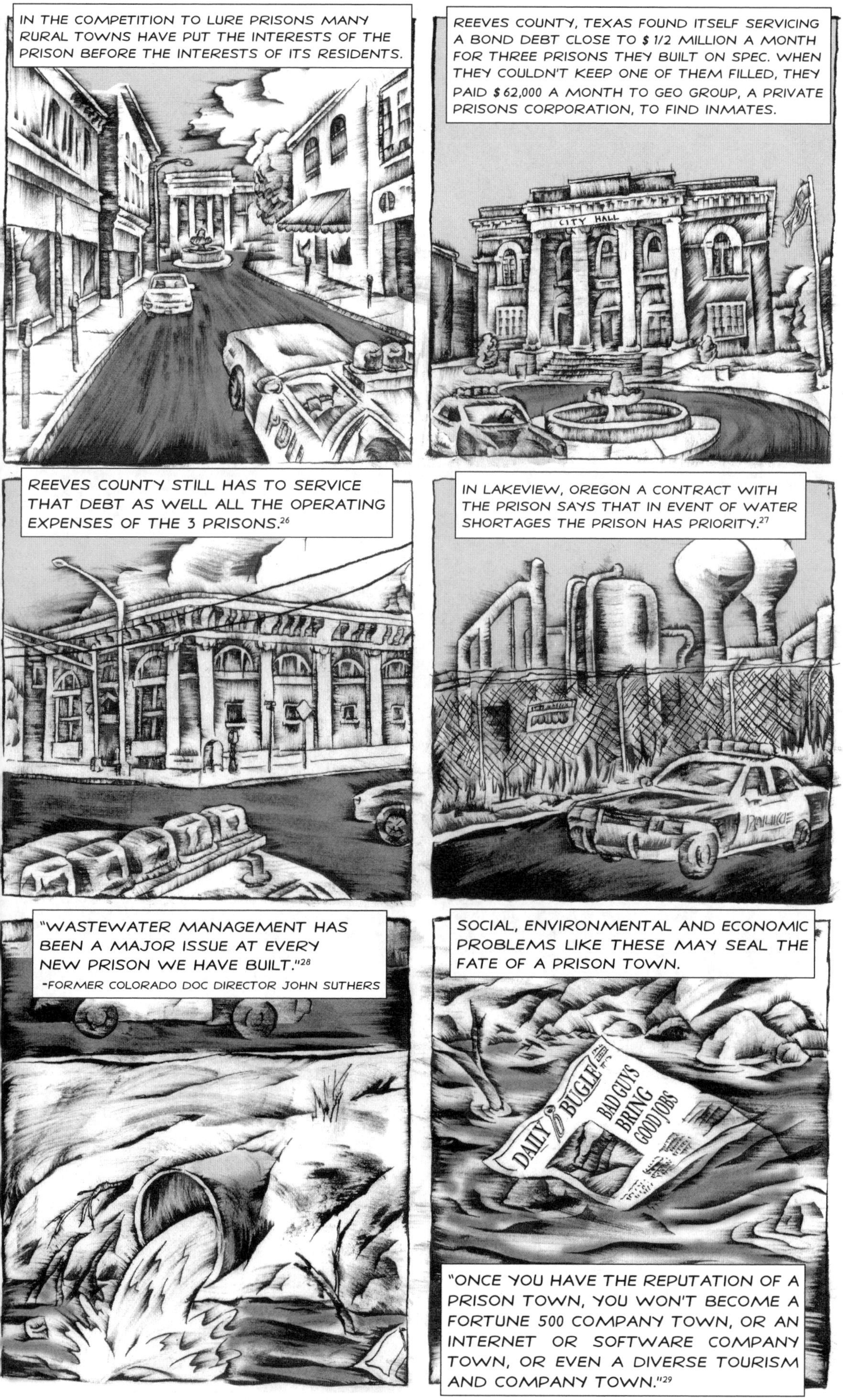
IN THE COMPETITION TO LURE PRISONS MANY RURAL TOWNS HAVE PUT THE INTERESTS OF THE PRISON BEFORE THE INTERESTS OF ITS RESIDENTS.
REEVES COUNTY, TEXAS FOUND ITSELF SERVICING A BOND DEBT CLOSE TO $ 1/2 MILLION A MONTH FOR THREE PRISONS THEY BUILT ON SPEC. WHEN THEY COULDN'T KEEP ONE OF THEM FILLED, THEY PAID $ 62,000 A MONTH TO GEO GROUP, A PRIVATE PRISONS CORPORATION, TO FIND INMATES.
CITY HALL
REEVES COUNTY STILL HAS TO SERVICE THAT DEBT AS WELL ALL THE OPERATING EXPENSES OF THE 3 PRISONS.[26]
IN LAKEVIEW, OREGON A CONTRACT WITH THE PRISON SAYS THAT IN EVENT OF WATER SHORTAGES THE PRISON HAS PRIORITY.[27]
"WASTEWATER MANAGEMENT HAS BEEN A MAJOR ISSUE AT EVERY NEW PRISON WE HAVE BUILT."[28]
-FORMER COLORADO DOC DIRECTOR JOHN SUTHERS
SOCIAL, ENVIRONMENTAL AND ECONOMIC PROBLEMS LIKE THESE MAY SEAL THE FATE OF A PRISON TOWN.
DAILY BUGLE
BAD GUYS BRING GOOD JOBS
"ONCE YOU HAVE THE REPUTATION OF A PRISON TOWN, YOU WON'T BECOME A FORTUNE 500 COMPANY TOWN, OR AN INTERNET OR SOFTWARE COMPANY TOWN, OR EVEN A DIVERSE TOURISM AND COMPANY TOWN."[29]

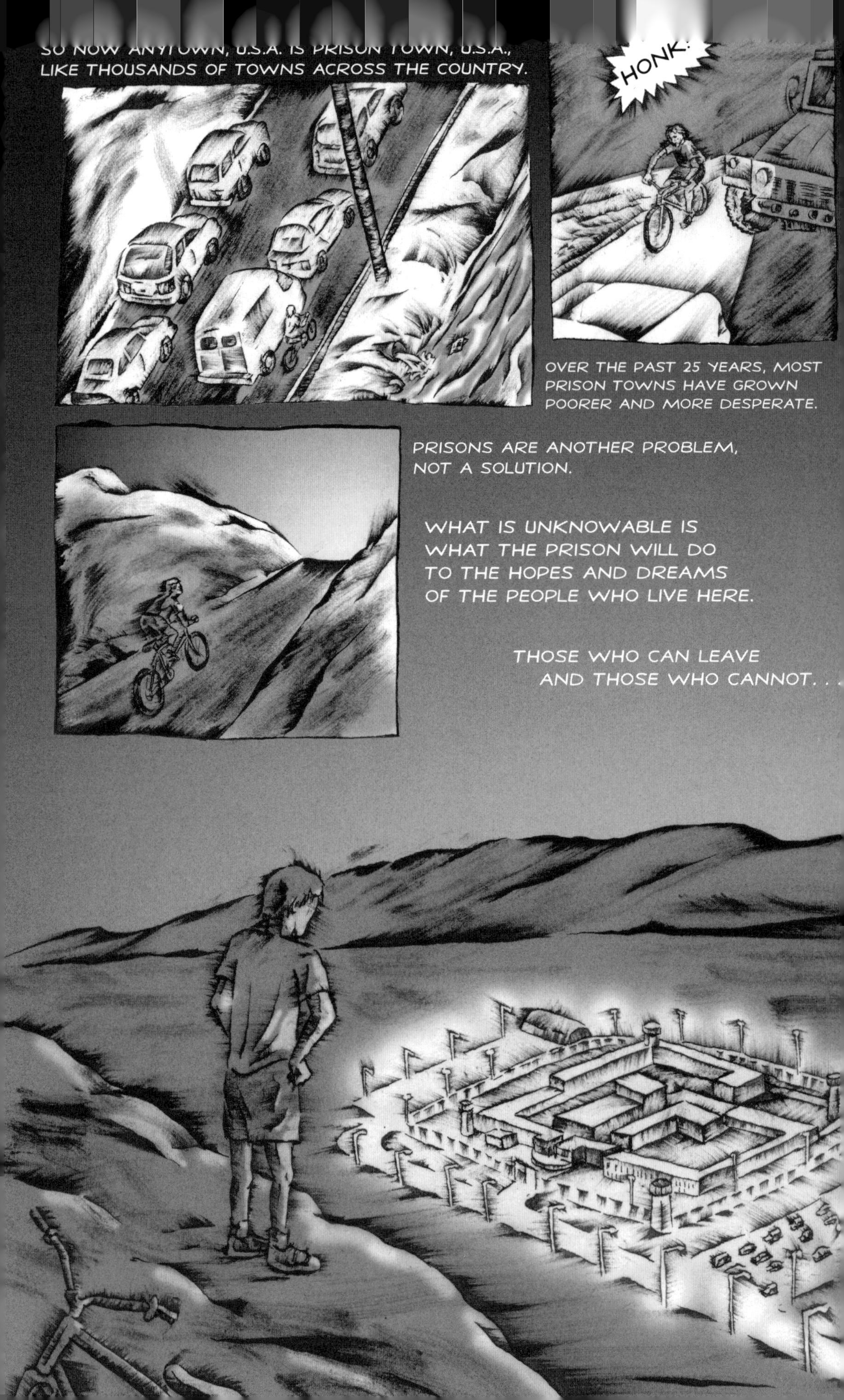
SO NOW ANYTOWN, U.S.A. IS PRISON TOWN, U.S.A.,
LIKE THOUSANDS OF TOWNS ACROSS THE COUNTRY.
HONK!
OVER THE PAST 25 YEARS, MOST PRISON TOWNS HAVE GROWN POORER AND MORE DESPERATE.
PRISONS ARE ANOTHER PROBLEM, NOT A SOLUTION.
WHAT IS UNKNOWABLE IS WHAT THE PRISON WILL DO TO THE HOPES AND DREAMS OF THE PEOPLE WHO LIVE HERE.
THOSE WHO CAN LEAVE
AND THOSE WHO CANNOT. . .

MILLION DOLLAR BLOCKS[30]

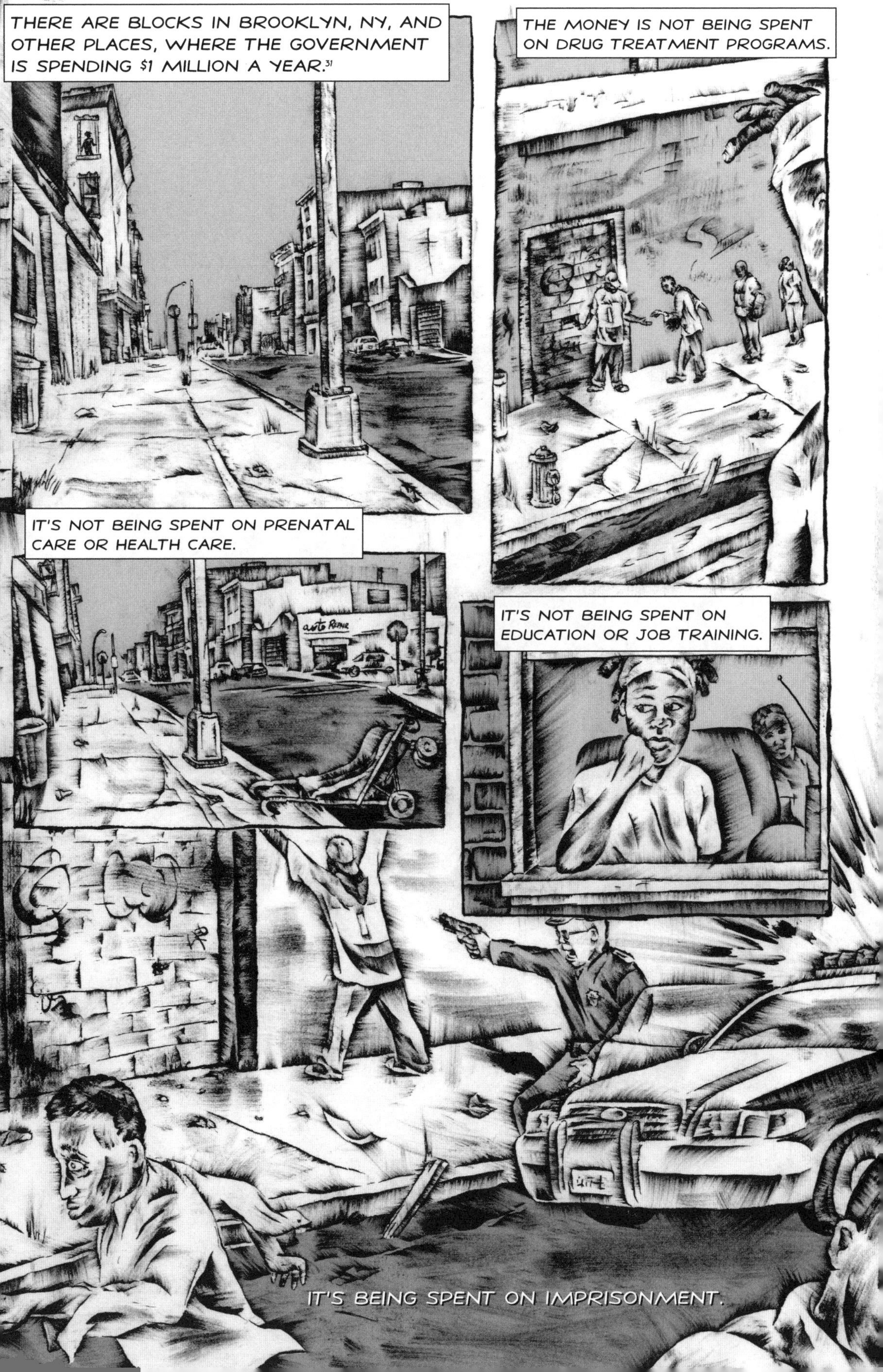
THERE ARE BLOCKS IN BROOKLYN, NY, AND OTHER PLACES, WHERE THE GOVERNMENT IS SPENDING $1 MILLION A YEAR.[31]
THE MONEY IS NOT BEING SPENT ON DRUG TREATMENT PROGRAMS.
IT'S NOT BEING SPENT ON PRENATAL CARE OR HEALTH CARE.
IT'S NOT BEING SPENT ON EDUCATION OR JOB TRAINING.
IT'S BEING SPENT ON IMPRISONMENT.

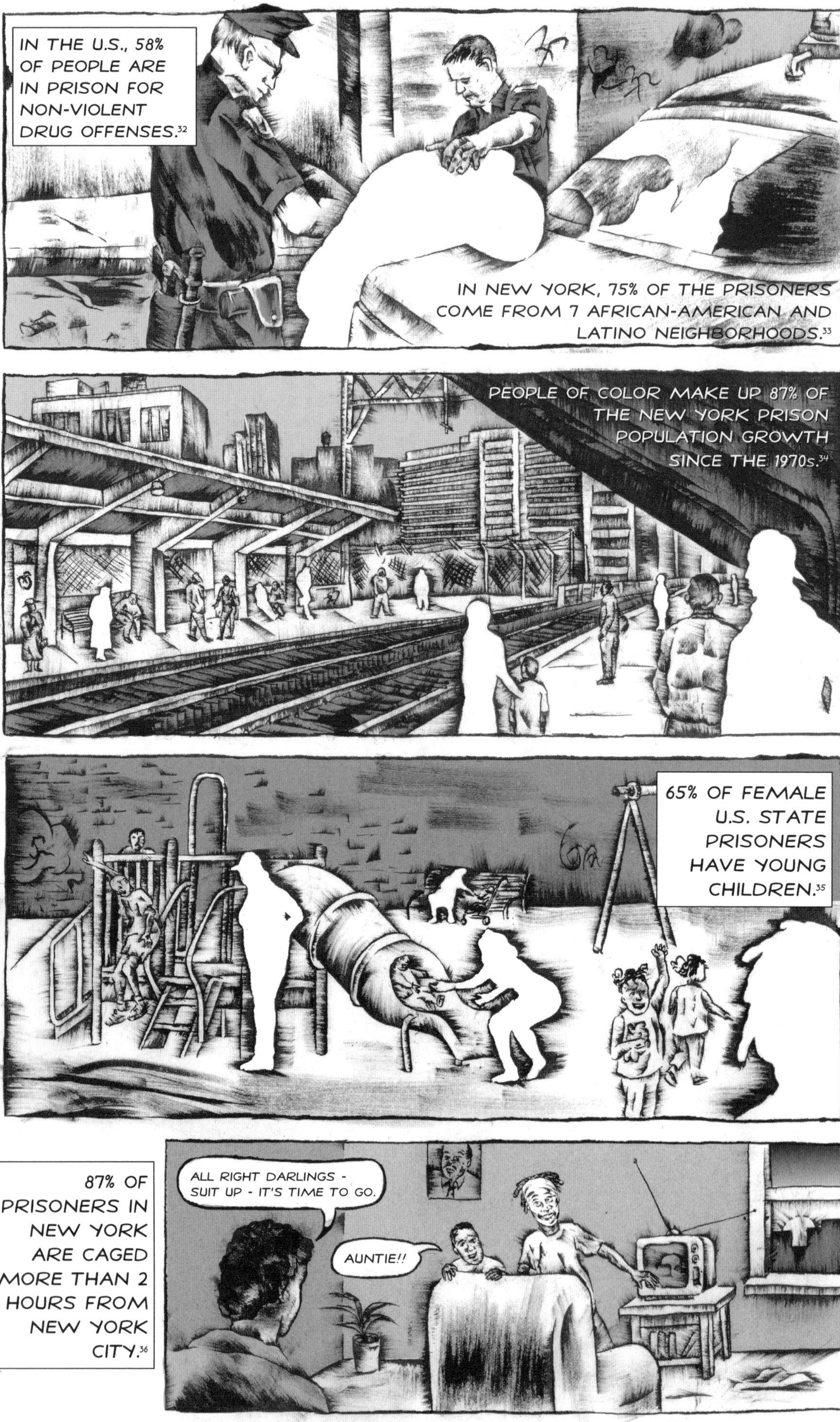
IN THE U.S., 58% OF PEOPLE ARE IN PRISON FOR NON-VIOLENT DRUG OFFENSES.[32]
IN NEW YORK, 75% OF THE PRISONERS COME FROM 7 AFRICAN-AMERICAN AND LATINO NEIGHBORHOODS.[33]
PEOPLE OF COLOR MAKE UP 87% OF THE NEW YORK PRISON POPULATION GROWTH SINCE THE 1970s.[34]
65% OF FEMALE U.S. STATE PRISONERS HAVE YOUNG CHILDREN.[35]
87% OF PRISONERS IN NEW YORK ARE CAGED MORE THAN 2 HOURS FROM NEW YORK CITY.[36]
ALL RIGHT DARLINGS - SUIT UP - IT'S TIME TO GO.
AUNTIE!!

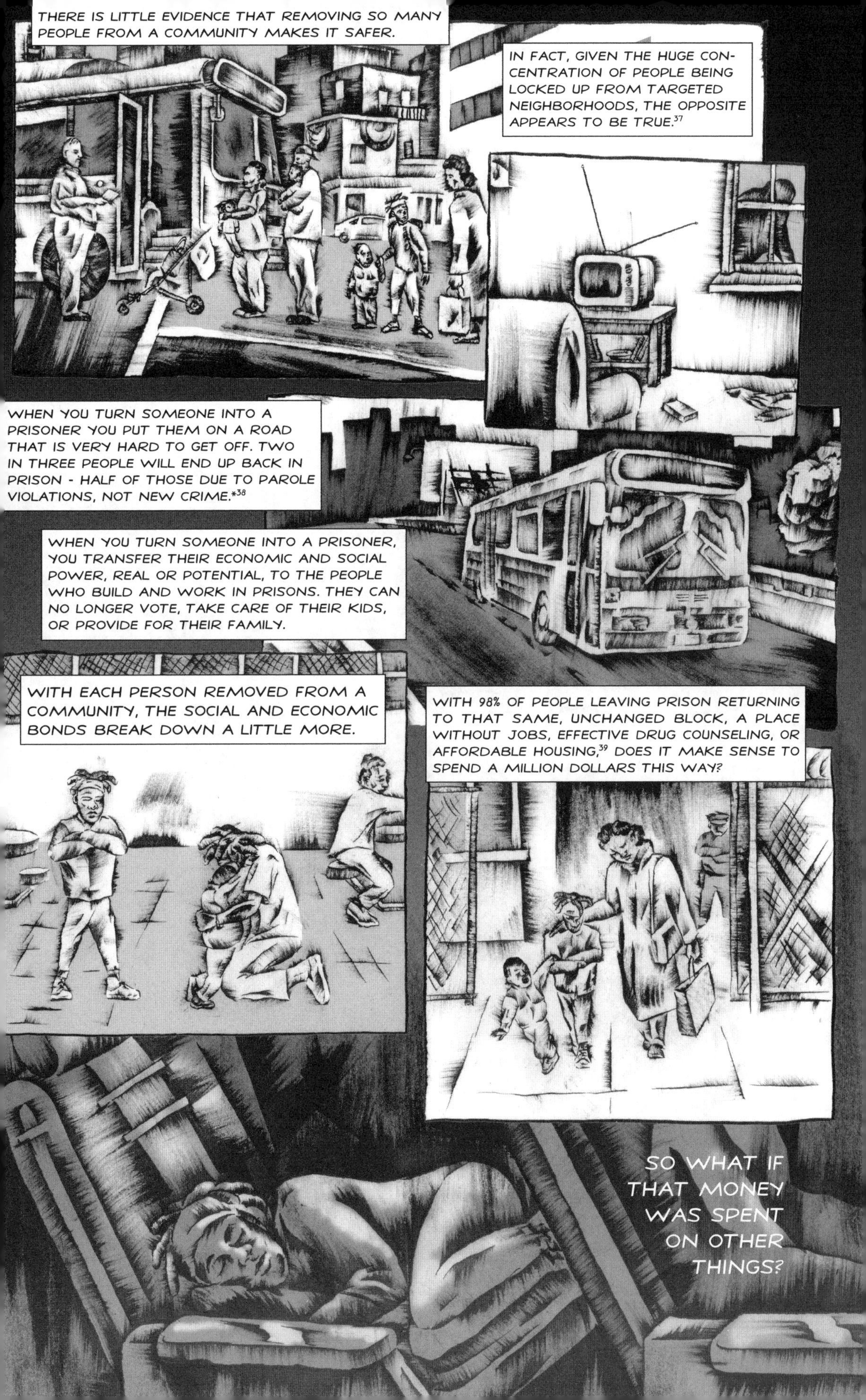
THERE IS LITTLE EVIDENCE THAT REMOVING SO MANY PEOPLE FROM A COMMUNITY MAKES IT SAFER.
IN FACT, GIVEN THE HUGE CONCENTRATION OF PEOPLE BEING LOCKED UP FROM TARGETED NEIGHBORHOODS, THE OPPOSITE APPEARS TO BE TRUE.[37]
WHEN YOU TURN SOMEONE INTO A PRISONER YOU PUT THEM ON A ROAD THAT IS VERY HARD TO GET OFF. TWO IN THREE PEOPLE WILL END UP BACK IN PRISON - HALF OF THOSE DUE TO PAROLE VIOLATIONS, NOT NEW CRIME.*[38]
WHEN YOU TURN SOMEONE INTO A PRISONER, YOU TRANSFER THEIR ECONOMIC AND SOCIAL POWER, REAL OR POTENTIAL, TO THE PEOPLE WHO BUILD AND WORK IN PRISONS. THEY CAN NO LONGER VOTE, TAKE CARE OF THEIR KIDS, OR PROVIDE FOR THEIR FAMILY.
WITH EACH PERSON REMOVED FROM A COMMUNITY, THE SOCIAL AND ECONOMIC BONDS BREAK DOWN A LITTLE MORE.
WITH 98% OF PEOPLE LEAVING PRISON RETURNING TO THAT SAME, UNCHANGED BLOCK, A PLACE WITHOUT JOBS, EFFECTIVE DRUG COUNSELING, OR AFFORDABLE HOUSING,[39] DOES IT MAKE SENSE TO SPEND A MILLION DOLLARS THIS WAY?
SO WHAT IF THAT MONEY WAS SPENT ON OTHER THINGS?

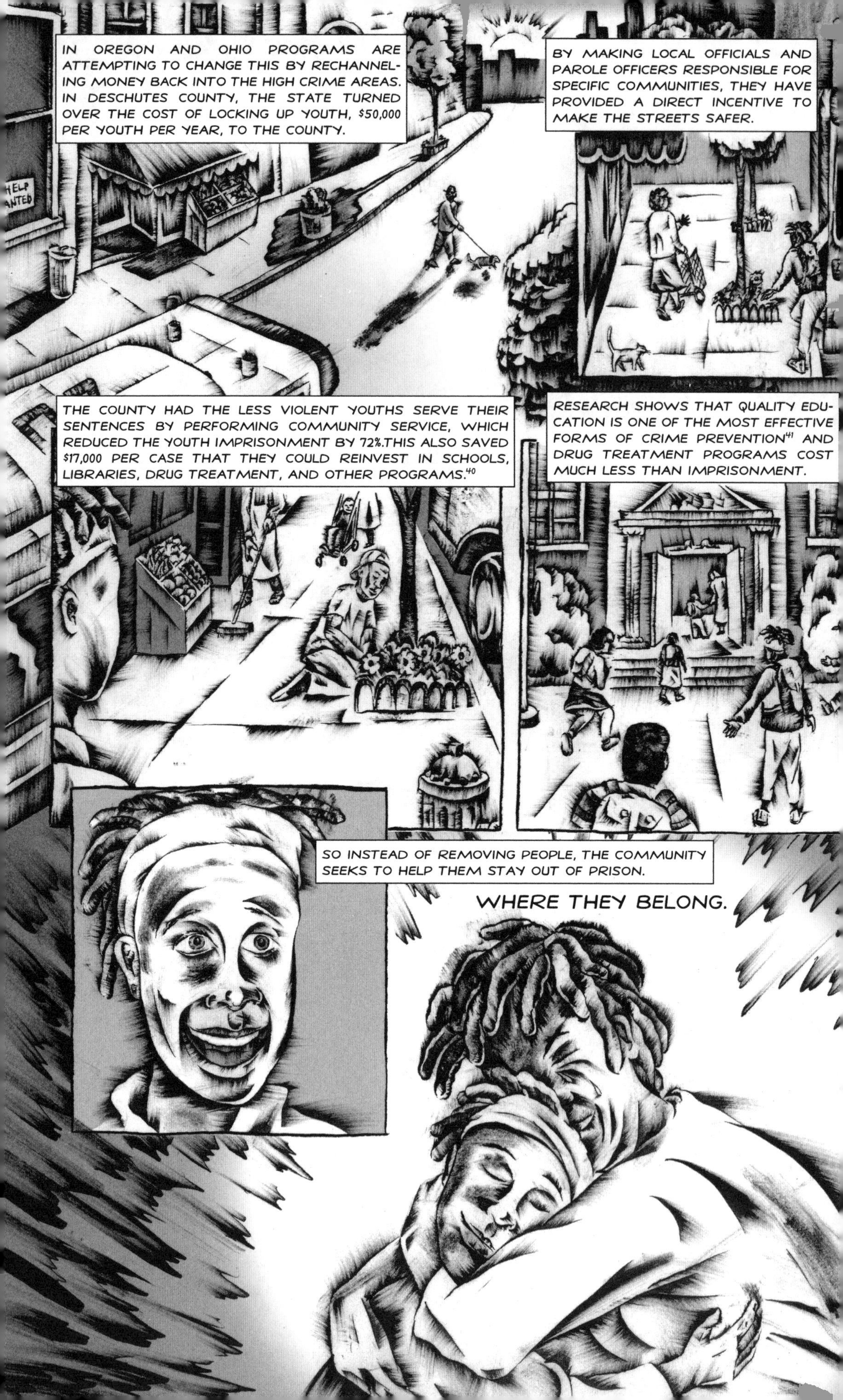

IN OREGON AND OHIO PROGRAMS ARE ATTEMPTING TO CHANGE THIS BY RECHANNELING MONEY BACK INTO THE HIGH CRIME AREAS. IN DESCHUTES COUNTY, THE STATE TURNED OVER THE COST OF LOCKING UP YOUTH, $50,000 PER YOUTH PER YEAR, TO THE COUNTY.
HELP WANTED
BY MAKING LOCAL OFFICIALS AND PAROLE OFFICERS RESPONSIBLE FOR SPECIFIC COMMUNITIES, THEY HAVE PROVIDED A DIRECT INCENTIVE TO MAKE THE STREETS SAFER.
THE COUNTY HAD THE LESS VIOLENT YOUTHS SERVE THEIR SENTENCES BY PERFORMING COMMUNITY SERVICE, WHICH REDUCED THE YOUTH IMPRISONMENT BY 72%.THIS ALSO SAVED $17,000 PER CASE THAT THEY COULD REINVEST IN SCHOOLS, LIBRARIES, DRUG TREATMENT, AND OTHER PROGRAMS.[40]
RESEARCH SHOWS THAT QUALITY EDUCATION IS ONE OF THE MOST EFFECTIVE FORMS OF CRIME PREVENTION[41] AND DRUG TREATMENT PROGRAMS COST MUCH LESS THAN IMPRISONMENT.
SO INSTEAD OF REMOVING PEOPLE, THE COMMUNITY SEEKS TO HELP THEM STAY OUT OF PRISON.
WHERE THEY BELONG.

GLOSSARY

oercive Migration: The movements of people from their eighborhoods, through the courts and jails to prison and ack. The concentrations of large numbers of prisoners in ertain rural prisons and the fact that their former homes are oncentrated in relatively few neighborhoods of urban poverty ads to huge impacts for the urban neighborhoods who deal ith constant turnover of their population and disrupt the nity of family and neighborhoods.

ommunity Reinvestment: The alternative to "Million Dollar locks." A program that redirects money spent on prisons to vestment on the blocks where current or formerly incarcer- ted men and women live, spending money on health care, b training, education, drug treatment and other services stead of incarceration.

orrections: (as in Department of Corrections) Term used ith no apparent sense of irony to describe government epartments in charge of prisons and the prison industry as whole.

riminalization: The process of making behaviors illegal or radically increasing the severity of the punishment. Also sed to describe the populations targeted by these policies, for xample, the criminalization of the homeless or of Black youth.

evelopment Subsidies: The opposite of mitigation funds. ubsidies are money paid by local or state governments to ttract or retain businesses. They can include city or state ax breaks, tax-advantaged financing, investment in roads, ousing or transportation funds for industry employees. Such ubsidies, often called "Corporate Welfare," rarely pay off for e town.

ndustry of Last Resort: Those industries who have trouble nding host communities because they are unpleasant neigh-

bors, for example: incinerators, prisons, concentrated animal feeding operations (CAFOs), toxic waste dumps. Industries of last resort seek communities desperate for jobs and tax revenues and where they believe people will not exercise their political power. For example: poor rural communities and inner city neighborhoods.

Million DollarBlock: A city block in which the state is spend- ing $1,000,000 or more to incarcerate former residents or to supervise the formerly incarcerated.

Mitigation: State money paid to local governments to pay the costs of siting including extending roads, sewage pipes, increased use of courts, etc. Mitigation offered by the state is usually far short of the real costs to the host community, leaving them in a deeper financial hole.

Police State: (1) Any state or country that relies primarily on police and prisons to control some or all of the population. (2) A state dependent on fear to keep people in order. (3) A place in which 'safety' is defined narrowly as security from acts of random violence rather than, for example, freedom to drive a car and not be stopped and searched for no reason.

Prison Industrial Complex: (often PIC): An informal or for- mal alliance of government bureaucrats, politicians, private industry, bankers, real estate developers and labor leaders who push criminalization, harsher sentences, more police and prisons which increases their political power and/or private incomes.

Siting: (Host) The process in which a prison (or other industry) chooses a location and convinces that community to welcome it. The community in which the prison is built is called the "host."

NOTES

: Peter Wagner, The Prison Index, 2003, pg. 5, www.prisonsucks.com
: Calvin Beale, "Cellular Rural Development: New Prisons in Rural and Small Town Areas in the 1990's," paper prepared for presentation at the annual meeting of the Rural Sociological Society, Albuquerque, New Mexico, August 18, 2001. From "Building a Prison Economy in Rural America," by Tracy Huling, pg. 2
: America's Diverse Family Farms, Agriculture Information Bulletin 769, Economic Research Service, US Department of Agriculture, May, 2001. From "Building a Prison Economy in Rural America," by Tracy Huling, pg. 1.
: Daniel Feldman, "20 Years of Prison Expansion: A Failing National Strategy," in Public Administration Review, Vol. 53, No. 6, November/ December, 1993. From "Building a Prison Economy in Rural America," by Tracy Huling, pg. 20
: Critical Resistance East California Prison Moratorium Project, New Forms of Environmental Racism, www.criticalresistance.org.
: Issues in Siting Correctional Facilities, Department Of Justice, pg. 17
: Prison Siting Forces Lawsuit Against U.S. DOJ, Western Prison Project, westernprisonproject.org
: Critical Resistance East & California Prison Moratorium Project, New Forms of Environmental Racism, www.criticalresistance.org.
: Issues in Siting Correctional Facilities, Department Of Justice, pg. 17
0: Sasha Abramsky, "Incarceration Inc," The Nation, 7/19/04.
1: David Jesse, "Cells For Rent," Times Herald, 4/11/04.
2: Richard P. Jones and Mary Zahn, "Decision to Build Prisons Moves Out of State's Hands," Milwaukee Journal Sentinel, 1/23/00.
3: Charles Westerberg, "Tough on Crime, Easy on Big Business," FightingBob. com, 6/26/03.
4: Richard P. Jones and Mary Zahn, "Decision to Build Prisons Moves Out of State's Hands," Milwaukee Journal Sentinel, 1/23/00.
5: Charlie Mitchell, "Competition is Fierce for an Unusual Asset: Prison Inmates," Vicksburg Post, 6/3/04.
6: "Web Site Connects Jail-Bed Renters with Sellers," www.correctionalnews.com, 7/10/04.
7: Peter Wagner, The Prison Index, 2003, pg. 35
8: Ruth Wilson Gilmore, Golden Gulag, University of California Press, 2005, from "Building a Prison Economy in Rural America" by Tracy Huling, pg. 6.
9: "Storm Raised by Plan for a California Prison" New York Times, 8/27/2000
20: Tracy Huling, "Building a Prison Economy in Rural America," pg. 7.
21: Douglas Clement, "Big House On The Prairie," Fedgazette, Federal

Reserve Bank of Minneapolis, Vol. 14, No. 1, January, 2002. From "Building a Prison Economy in Rural America," by Tracy Huling, pg. 7.
22: John K. Wiley, "Study: Hosting Prisons Could Harm Small Towns' Economic Prospects," Associated Press, 7/17/04.
23: Tracy Huling, "Prisons as a Growth Industry in Rural America: An Exploratory Discussion of the Effects on Young African American Men in the Inner Cities," 05/15/99.
24: Joelle Fraser, "An American Seduction: Portrait of a Prison Town," in Herivel and Wright, Prison Nation, 73–84.
25: Ibid
26: Sasha Abramsky, "Incarceration Inc," The Nation, 7/19/04.
27: Prison Siting Forces Lawsuit Against U.S. DOJ, Western Prison Project.
28: Stephen Raher, "Research Memo Re: Economic Impacts of Rural Prisons," Colorado Criminal Justice Reform Coalition. 5/22/2003.
29: Tracy Huling, "Building a Prison Economy in Rural America," pg. 12.
30: This chapter is heavily indebted to Dina R. Rose and Todd R. Clear's paper "Incarceration, Reentry, and Social Capital: Social Networks in the Balance," 12/01.
31: Susan B. Tucker and Eric Cadora, "Justice Reinvestment," Ideas for an Open Society, vol. 3 number 3, 11/03, pg. 2.
32: Peter Wagner, The Prison Index, 2003, pg. 27.
33: Tracy Huling, "Prisons as a Growth Industry in Rural America: An Exploratory Discussion of the Effects on Young African American Men in the Inner Cities." www.prisonpolicy.org/scans/prisons_as_rural_growth.shtml
34: Peter Wagner, The Prison Index, 2003, pg. 35.
35: Ibid, pg. 31.
36: Ibid, pg. 26.
37: Dina R.Rose and Todd R. Clear, "Incarceration, Reentry and Social Capital: Social Networks in the Balance," 2002.
38: Susan B. Tucker and Eric Cadora, "Justice Reinvestment," Ideas for an Open Society, vol. 3 number 3, 11/03, pg. 2. *Conditions of probation can be violated for a missed curfew or a "dirty" urine.
39: Ibid, pg. 3
40: Susan B. Tucker and Eric Cadora, "From Prisons to Parks in Oregon," Ideas for an Open Society, vol. 3 number 3, 11/03, pg. 2.
41: Tracy Huling, "Prisons as a Growth Industry in Rural America: An Exploratory Discussion of the Effects on Young African American Men in the Inner Cities." www.prisonpolicy.org/scans/prisons_as_rural_growth.shtml

NATIONAL AVERAGE
COST TO IMPRISON
A PERSON FOR ONE
YEAR: $29,041

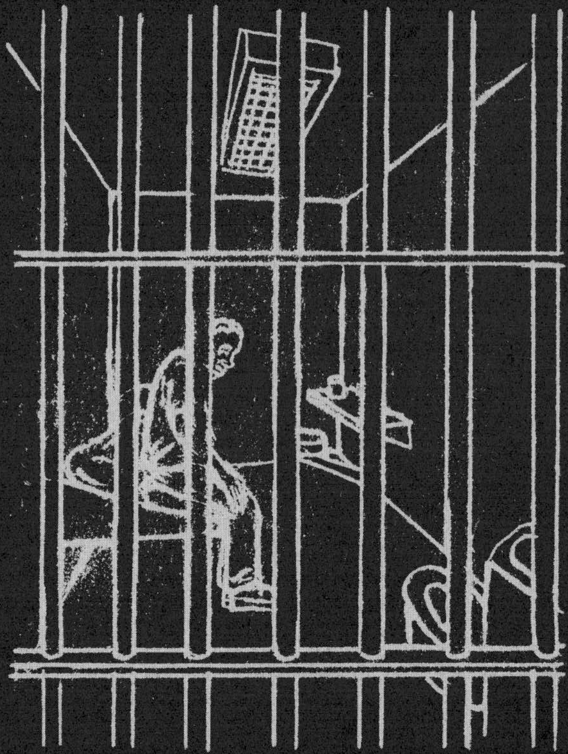

the cost of a cage

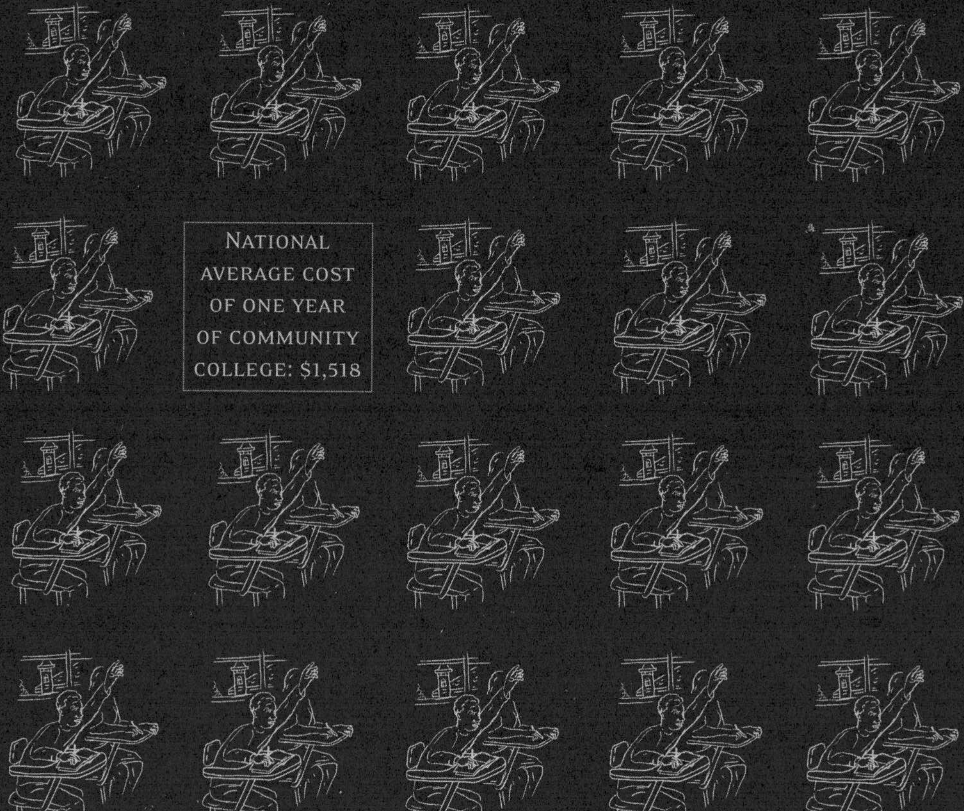
NATIONAL
AVERAGE COST
OF ONE YEAR
OF COMMUNITY
COLLEGE: $1,518

readers respond

I read the comic books of The Real Cost of Prisons Project to educate myself about the human consequences of imprisonment in the United States, so I am delighted to see that these will now be published in a single volume for the general public. The drawings and texts combine powerful factual data with personal stories which cannot fail to touch the heart. They dig beneath the obvious—the dehumanization, the racism, the tearing apart of families, the absurdity of the "war on drugs"—to show how poverty and desperation bring people into a system which then exploits them for the profit of a prison-industrial complex. I cannot think of a better way to arouse the public to the cruelties of the prison system than to make this book widely available.

–HOWARD ZINN

In our anti-incarceration work in the deep rural south of Louisiana, these comic books turned out to be a big hit with the folks we do outreach with, typically poor children and families of color, targeted by the juvenile justice system in Louisiana. They helped explain in simple terms what can be a difficult issue to explain, especially in the few minutes you may have with a potential new member. These comic books were of great value to all of us in Louisiana!

–GRACE BAUER
Statewide Community Organizer
Families and Friends of Louisiana's Incarcerated Children

The Real Cost of Prisons comics are among the most transformative pieces of information that the youth get to read. We take it with us to detention centers, group homes, youth shelters and social justice organizing projects. Everywhere we go we see youth nodding with agreement and getting excited to see their reality validated in print. And when they get that acknowledgment that the system is as complicated, targeting and marginalizing as they know it to be, they start wondering how they can make changes to their lives and to the world. The Real Cost of Prisons helps youth know what's up and gives them the push they need to get active in the struggle to make interpersonal and community-wide change.

–SHIRA HASSAN
Co-Director
Young Women's Empowerment Project, Chicago, IL

The format of the comic books makes complicated, interrelated concepts accessible to the layperson. If this country is to end its addiction to incarceration, this is just the sort of well-researched material that our citizens must understand.

–CHARLES SULLIVAN
Executive Director
Citizens United for Rehabilitation of Errants (CURE)

An accessible, compelling, and informative look at America's answer to many of our social welfare and public health problems—lock 'em up. This costly and ineffective approach is destroying families and undermining American values of liberty, compassion, and progress. These comics have been enthusiastically received by prisoners, students, families, social justice activists, legal advocates, academics and policy makers alike. Feedback has consistently been that the comics are an extremely effective education and organizing tool. National Advocates for Pregnant Women has found them to be an extremely valuable resource, helping people to gain quickly a comprehensive overview of the truth about prisons, jails and the human suffering caused by a dangerous and counterproductive war on drugs and low-income families.

–LYNN M. PALTROW, JD
Executive Director
National Advocates for Pregnant Women
New York, NY

Each comic book comes at the prison industry from a different angle and provides the readers with a depth that belies its comic format. They offer a terrific comprehensive overview of the problems we face as a result of mass incarceration. It's exciting to have a digestible format that teaches people that far from making us safer, the prison industry destroys families and individuals, doesn't support communities, and is bad public health and poor long-term economics.

–ALLAN CLEAR
Executive Director
The Harm Reduction Coalition

We have used all three of the comic books as educational and organizing tools in our work challenging pollution and prisons. Our agency offers opportunities for self-determination among those most adversely and disproportionately impacted by this country's reliance on mass incarceration and fossil fuels: our young people. So these creative tools for social change have ventured with us into local facilities for incarcerated youth, public school classrooms which we identify as the start of the "school to prison" pipeline, and the streets of our "enlightened community" where we connect the dots between 500-year-old issues of prejudice, inequality, oppression, and discrimination with the increased use of policing, supervision, detention, and incarceration nationwide and abroad. These comic books are a popular and potent resource!

–LESLIE F. JONES, ESQ.
Executive Director
Southern Tier Advocacy & Mitigation Project
Ithaca, NY

The RCPP series brings to light the stark realities of the U.S. prison system. The comic-book format makes complex issues such as the war on drugs, prison economics, and family impacts accessible to a broad audience. By doing so, it is helping to build a new generation of change agents for reform.

–MARC MAUER
Executive Director
The Sentencing Project
Washington, DC

As I sat reading this comic book, I slowly felt my heart get heavy and the tears well up in my eyes. The statistics alone can make a person want to cry, throw up, and rip their hair out all at the same time. When you add real-life stories, with names and histories, it becomes even more painful. And truthfully, the most painful part of this for me is that every single woman who is in the prison system (and a large percentage of those who are not in the prison system) has a story similar to these stories.

I really hope that I can turn my emotions from reading this book into actions than can help prevent future stories like those told in the book.

–NADIA SCHREIBER
Feminist Theory Class
NYC Lab High School

The real cost of prisons: a simple enough concept for a complex reality. The cost is measured in many ways: in the lost talents of those who are spending years of their lives behind bars, shut away from families and communities; in the pain suffered by those whose lives are damaged or destroyed by crime; in the frustration and wasted energy of those who devote their lives to "protecting" society and "correcting" the convicted, but who see that the impact of their labor is often negligible, if not negative; and in our vast public corrections expenditures, which draw resources away from much-needed social investment.

We can do better than locking our fellow citizens in cages. We have the resources, we have the creativity, and we have the ability to enact real justice. All we need now is the political will. And it all starts with realizing what the problems are. The Real Cost of Prisons Project goes a long way in opening a window to our understanding of the issues of crime and justice affecting us all. Through the creativity of this unique medium, the issues are brought to life and made accessible to people of all ages. I have used these comic books in my classes inside prison, which include both incarcerated students and non-incarcerated university students. Everyone appreciates the depth of the content, the richness of the style, and the complexity that is rendered through a few deceptively simple strokes of a pen. They speak volumes.

–LORI POMPA
Founder and Director
The Inside-Out Prison Exchange Program
A National Program based at
Temple University
Philadelphia, PA

From the moment I saw the first comic book released by The Real Cost of Prisons Project, I knew we had a powerful way to reach and educate folks. There is not an event we attend that the comic books aren't present. They are always the most sought-after item we bring. Those of us with the job of educating our misinformed public applaud The Real Cost of Prisons comics and look for more in the future.

–GERI SILVA
Families to Amend California's
Three Strikes (FACTS)
Los Angeles, CA

I came into the Pennsylvania Prison System in 1970 when there were seven prisons. There are now 26 state Correctional Institutions in Pennsylvania, and three more under construction. Race and poverty form the foundation of the Prison Pipeline. The politics of police systems, courts, and the prison system are a manifestation of the racism and the classism which govern so many lives in this country.

Young men of color have been discarded as waste products of the technological revolution. I don't believe that it is an accident that poor people who are perceived as economic liabilities have now been turned into a major economic asset in the creation of this prison job market.

I believe in book form, the comic books will reach a much wider audience. There is an audience in grade schools, junior and senior high schools for youth who do not really understand what can put them at risk and have life-long consequences.

–MICHAEL "SMOKEY" WILSON
Lifers Inc. / End Violence Projects
Graterford, PA

———

In 2004, I first started using *Prison Town-Paying the Price* to help in the fight against privatized prisons in Lamar, CO. The Concerned Citizens of Lamar put the comic books to outstanding use. We eventually won a ferocious battle with municipal authorities who were determined to site the prison. Distribution of the comic books helped them defeat the proposal.

That same year, GEO (international private prison corporation) came back to Kansas for another try to privatize prisons. When a surprise hearing was scheduled for the House Appropriations Committee, I sent each member a wealth of materials. I also sent each of them the comic book.

On hearing day in the committee room, I was collating new stacks of documents I'd brought with me and extremely occupied. Finally I looked up. There was over half the Committee READING *PRISON TOWN*! The proposal went nowhere!

Since that hearing, almost three years ago, I have made the comic books a centerpiece of community education and organization in state after state around the country. When I send *Prison Town* out to communities, I am invariably contacted by local recipients expressing their immense gratitude and almost always asking the same question: "How many more can we get?"

–FRANK SMITH
National Field Organizer
Private Corrections Institute
Bluff City, KS

———

It's hard to find good written material on the prison-industrial-complex that works with teenagers. It's either personal anecdote with a heavy "don't make the same mistake I did" focus, or in academic language way over the kids' heads. Both *Prisoners of the War on Drugs* and *Prison Town* combine illustrated stories with analysis in ways that push teenagers to think critically about the issues.

–JODY SOKOLOWER
Teacher
Berkeley, CA

———

The comic books capture the nuts and bolts of who is incarcerated and how they got there. Poverty, drug abuse, sexual abuse, untreated mental illness, HIV, broken families: these are the stories of incarceration we all need to hear. The comics speak in language that informs, provokes questions, and is not easy to dismiss.

If you work as a midwife, the odds are great that women in your care have been incarcerated, or that their mothers, fathers, children or partners have been. These comics give voice to their stories, and show the ripples, near and distant, that are a part of our system of incarceration today.

I have given the comic books to nursing students who request to come with me to the jail to see women patients. The response is invariably, "Wow," then silence, then, "I never realized....."

–DONNA JACKSON-KÖHLIN
CNM, MSN, Baystate Midwifery and Women's Health, which provides health care to women incarcerated at the Women's Correctional Center Chicopee, MA

The comic books are a must read and great tool. They allow us to see ourselves as part of the picture, thereby aiding our discussion as we attempt to flesh-out and address the maladies that pervade our communities today like toxic fumes.

–ERNEST YAQIN NEDAB
Graterford Prison, PA

Occasionally one comes across a work which lights up a whole era as by a lightning flash. These books had such an effect on me. I have used the comic books during the classes I teach to prisoners. In a prison setting these books can help bring about personal growth via group discussion since most prisoners are familiar with the situations and stories described and shown in the books. It is my hope that the views and information presented in the comic books will help others to further develop their own way of how to put the new learning they gain from the comic books into practice. The comic books are a good beginning. This type of learning requires a lifelong commitment to continual inquiry and knowledge, understanding and insight. These books will be helpful to community leaders, schools, colleges and churches in provoking a needed conversation.

–TIYO ATTALLAH SALAH-EL
S.C.I. Dallas, PA

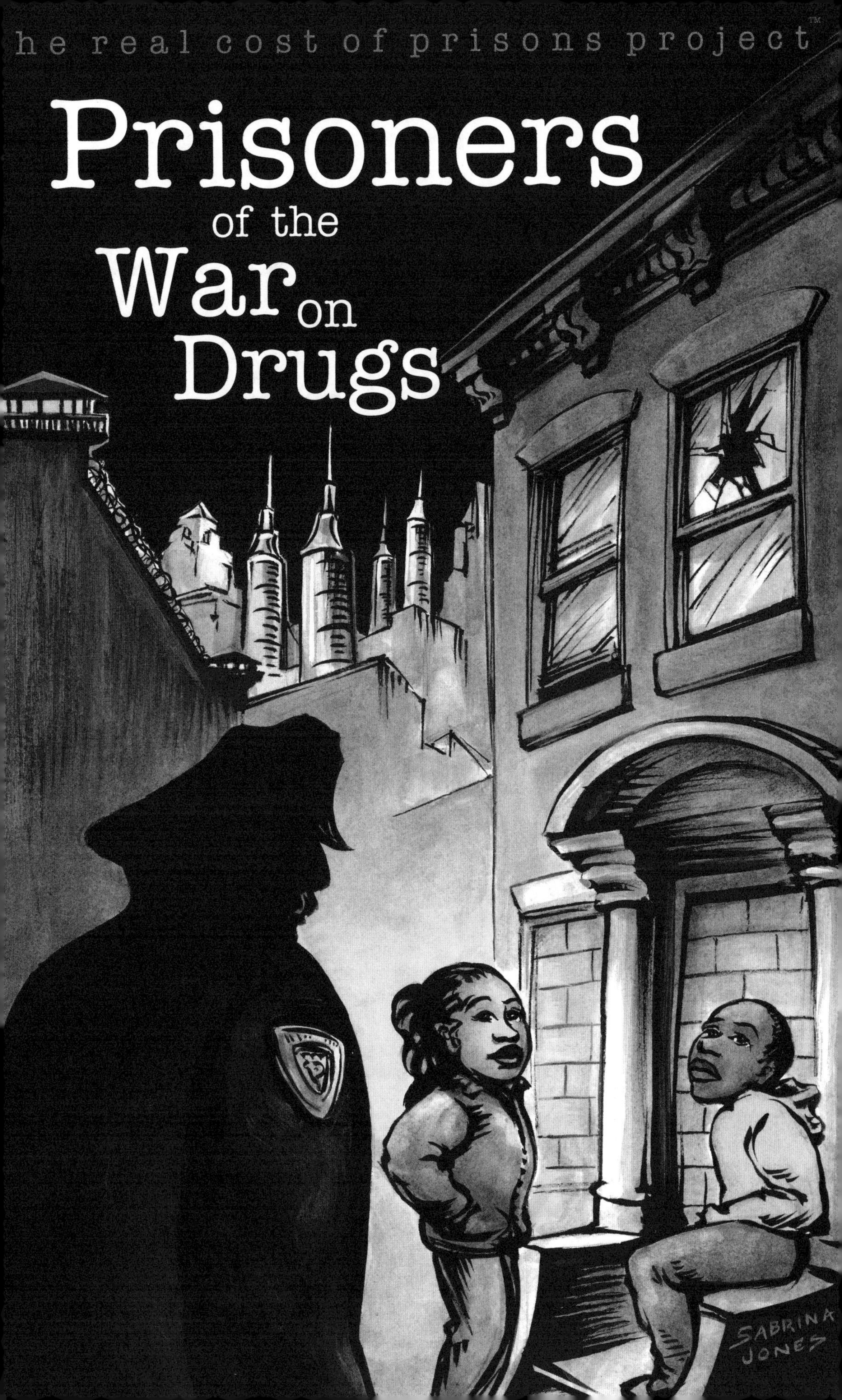
he real cost of prisons project™
Prisoners
of the
War on
Drugs
SABRINA JONES

www.realcostofprisons.org • info@realcostofprisons.org

Prisoners
of the War on Drugs

Artist: Sabrina Jones
Writers: Sabrina Jones, Ellen Miller-Mack & Lois Ahrens
Real Cost of the War on Drugs workshop writer/presenter: Mark Brenner
Art Direction & Design: Chris Shadoian
Real Cost of Prisons Project Director: Lois Ahrens

The Real Cost of Prisons Project brings together prison/justice policy activists with political economists to create workshops and materials which explore both the immediate and long-term costs of mass incarceration on the individual, her/his family, community and the nation.

Two additional comic books are part of this series: *Prison Town: Paying the Price* and *Prisoners of Hard Times: Women and Children.* If you would like copies of these comic books to assist your group in its organizing work, contact Lois Ahrens. Or you can go to www.realcostofprisons.org and download the entire series.

The Real Cost of Prisons Project is an activity of The Sentencing Project, a Washington, DC based non-profit dedicated to reducing over-reliance on incarceration. The Real Cost of Prisons Project is supported by a grant from the Community Advocacy Project of the Open Society Institute.

The characters in these stories are fictional, but their experiences are taken from actual case histories.

THANK YOU

Families Against Mandatory Minimums (FAMM), Tina Reynolds, Joanne Archibald, Eric Cadora, Todd Clear, Dina Rose, N.C. Christopher Couch, James Heinz, Marc Mauer, Malcolm Young, Raquiba LaBrie, William Johnston & Helena Huang.

Write to us at 5 Warfield Place, Northampton, MA 01060. Printed in Canada.
For more work by Sabrina Jones, please visit www.sabrinaland.com

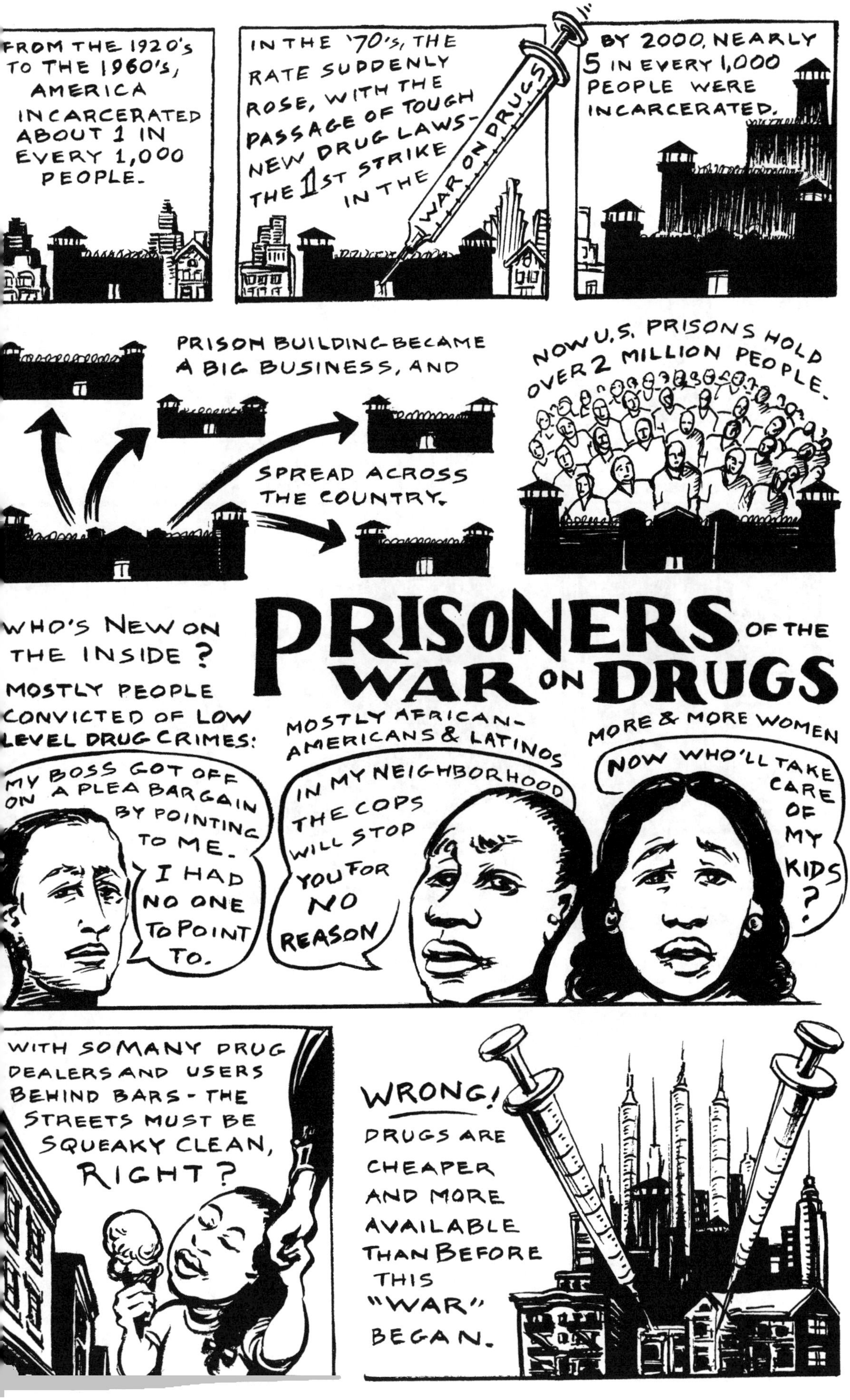

FROM THE 1920's TO THE 1960's, AMERICA INCARCERATED ABOUT 1 IN EVERY 1,000 PEOPLE.
IN THE '70's, THE RATE SUDDENLY ROSE, WITH THE PASSAGE OF TOUGH NEW DRUG LAWS- THE 1ST STRIKE IN THE
WAR ON DRUGS
BY 2000, NEARLY 5 IN EVERY 1,000 PEOPLE WERE INCARCERATED.
PRISON BUILDING BECAME A BIG BUSINESS, AND
SPREAD ACROSS THE COUNTRY.
NOW U.S. PRISONS HOLD OVER 2 MILLION PEOPLE.
PRISONERS OF THE WAR ON DRUGS
WHO'S NEW ON THE INSIDE? MOSTLY PEOPLE CONVICTED OF LOW LEVEL DRUG CRIMES:
MY BOSS GOT OFF ON A PLEA BARGAIN BY POINTING TO ME.
I HAD NO ONE TO POINT TO.
MOSTLY AFRICAN-AMERICANS & LATINOS
IN MY NEIGHBORHOOD THE COPS WILL STOP YOU FOR NO REASON
MORE & MORE WOMEN
NOW WHO'LL TAKE CARE OF MY KIDS?
WITH SO MANY DRUG DEALERS AND USERS BEHIND BARS - THE STREETS MUST BE SQUEAKY CLEAN, RIGHT?
WRONG!
DRUGS ARE CHEAPER AND MORE AVAILABLE THAN BEFORE THIS "WAR" BEGAN.

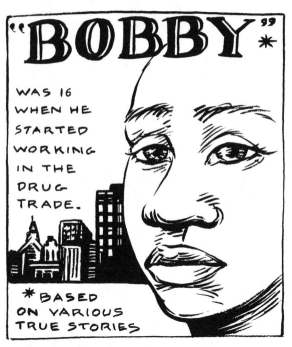

"BOBBY" *

WAS 16 WHEN HE STARTED WORKING IN THE DRUG TRADE.

*BASED ON VARIOUS TRUE STORIES

HE LIVED IN A SMALL APARTMENT IN CHICAGO

WITH HIS MOM, HIS TWO LITTLE BROTHERS, AND HIS SISTER.

EVERY DAY HIS MOTHER RODE THE BUS

3 HOURS ROUND TRIP TO WORK IN A MALL IN THE SUBURBS

LET'S GO, GUYS! GET READY FOR SCHOOL

THEY ALREADY GREW OUT OF THEIR CLOTHES AGAIN!

HI KIDS, I'M HOME

HI MOM

I CAN'T ASK HER FOR ANY MORE MONEY

HIS FIRST JOB WAS SIMPLE:

YOU JUST WHISTLE WHEN YOU SEE THE COPS.

BOBBY MADE $300 A WEEK CASH

& STAYED IN SCHOOL

BOBBY GOT ARRESTED WITH A BUNCH OF HIS "BUDDIES."

WE CAN LOCK YOU UP FOREVER

OR YOU CAN TELL US WHO RUNS THIS WHOLE OPERATION.

THE OTHERS BOBBY THEIR CLAIMED WAS KINGPIN.

THE PROSECUTOR ESTIMATED THE AMOUNT OF DRUGS

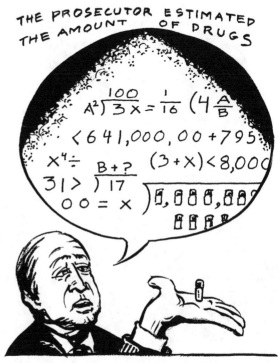

$$A^2 \overline{)\,3x\,}\,\frac{100}{} = \frac{1}{16} \left(4\frac{A}{B}\right.$$

$$< 641,000,00 + 795$$

$$X^4 \div \frac{B+?}{31 >\ )\,17} \quad (3+X) < 8,000$$

$$00 = X \quad \overline{)\,5,000,000}$$

A JURY FOUND BOBBY GUILTY OF CONSPIRACY FOR ALL THE ESTIMATED SALES OF HIS SO-CALLED EMPIRE.

HIS ACCUSERS AVOIDED TRIAL AND GOT REDUCED SENTENCES.

BOBBY WAS 18 YEARS OLD WHEN HE BEGAN SERV- ING 15 TO LIFE.

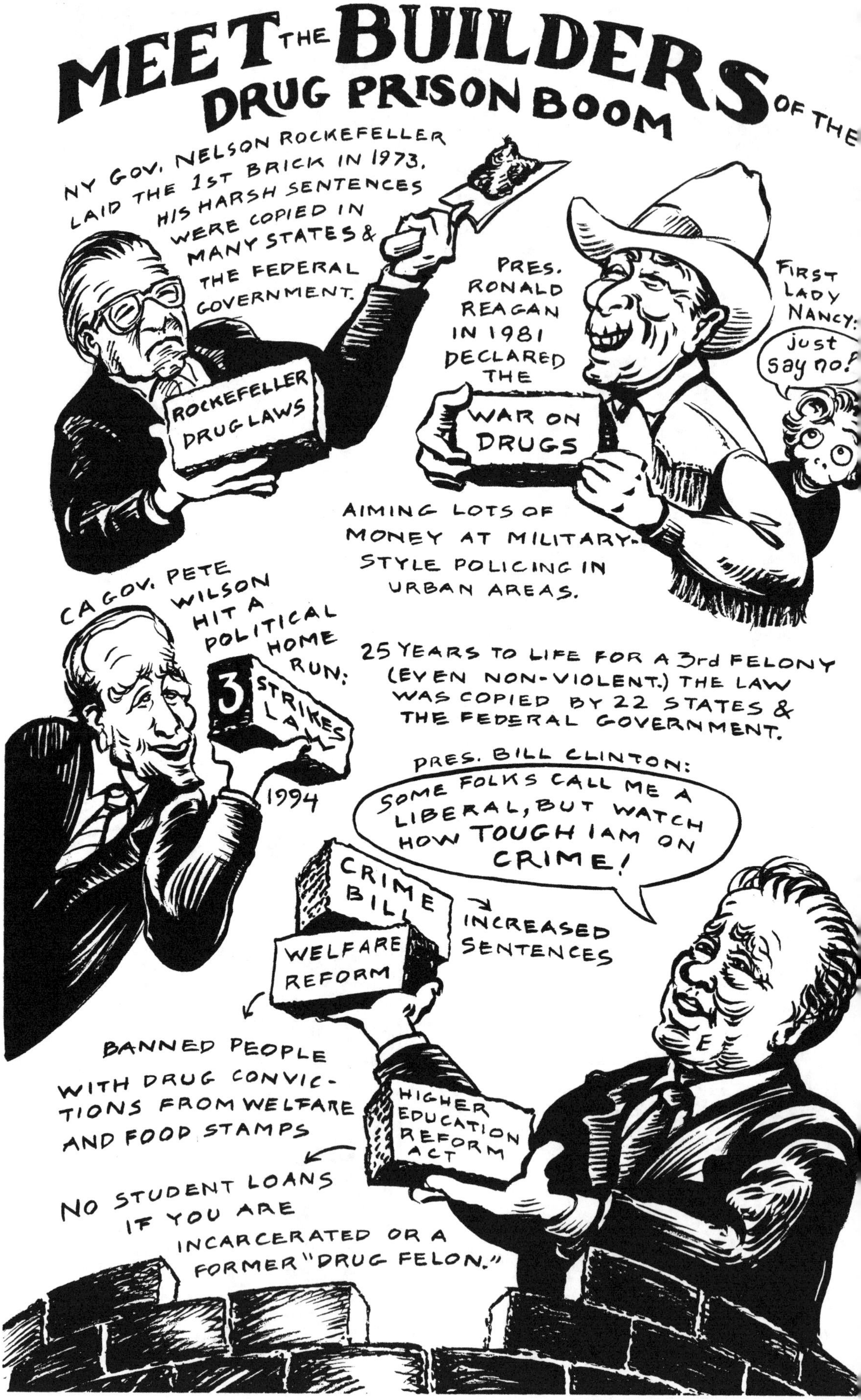
MEET THE BUILDERS OF THE DRUG PRISON BOOM
NY GOV. NELSON ROCKEFELLER LAID THE 1st BRICK IN 1973. HIS HARSH SENTENCES WERE COPIED IN MANY STATES & THE FEDERAL GOVERNMENT.
ROCKEFELLER DRUG LAWS
PRES. RONALD REAGAN IN 1981 DECLARED THE
WAR ON DRUGS
FIRST LADY NANCY:
just say no!
AIMING LOTS OF MONEY AT MILITARY-STYLE POLICING IN URBAN AREAS.
CA GOV. PETE WILSON HIT A POLITICAL HOME RUN:
3 STRIKES LAW
1994
25 YEARS TO LIFE FOR A 3rd FELONY (EVEN NON-VIOLENT.) THE LAW WAS COPIED BY 22 STATES & THE FEDERAL GOVERNMENT.
PRES. BILL CLINTON:
SOME FOLKS CALL ME A LIBERAL, BUT WATCH HOW TOUGH I AM ON CRIME!
CRIME BILL
INCREASED SENTENCES
WELFARE REFORM
BANNED PEOPLE WITH DRUG CONVIC-TIONS FROM WELFARE AND FOOD STAMPS
HIGHER EDUCATION REFORM ACT
NO STUDENT LOANS IF YOU ARE INCARCERATED OR A FORMER "DRUG FELON."

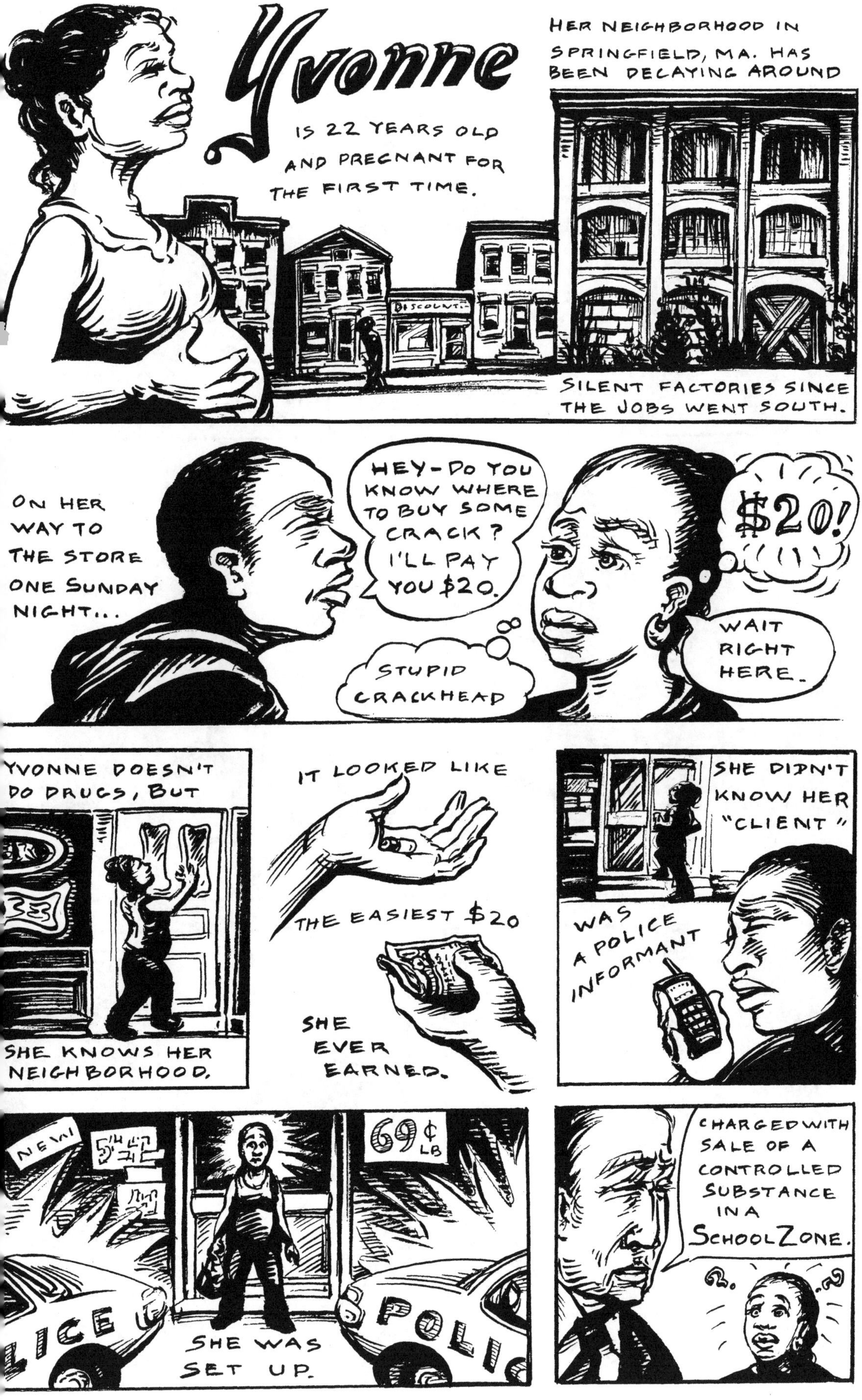
Yvonne
IS 22 YEARS OLD AND PREGNANT FOR THE FIRST TIME.
DISCOUNT
HER NEIGHBORHOOD IN SPRINGFIELD, MA. HAS BEEN DECAYING AROUND
SILENT FACTORIES SINCE THE JOBS WENT SOUTH.
ON HER WAY TO THE STORE ONE SUNDAY NIGHT...
HEY-DO YOU KNOW WHERE TO BUY SOME CRACK? I'LL PAY YOU $20.
$20!
STUPID CRACKHEAD
WAIT RIGHT HERE.
YVONNE DOESN'T DO DRUGS, BUT
SHE KNOWS HER NEIGHBORHOOD.
IT LOOKED LIKE
THE EASIEST $20
SHE EVER EARNED.
SHE DIDN'T KNOW HER "CLIENT"
WAS A POLICE INFORMANT
NEW
69¢ LB
LICE
POLI
SHE WAS SET UP.
CHARGED WITH SALE OF A CONTROLLED SUBSTANCE IN A SCHOOL ZONE.

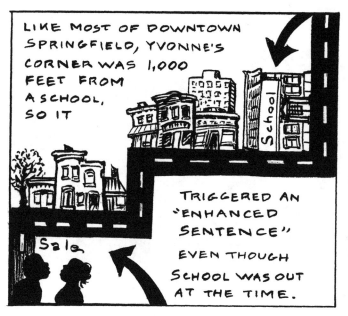

LIKE MOST OF DOWNTOWN SPRINGFIELD, YVONNE'S CORNER WAS 1,000 FEET FROM A SCHOOL, SO IT

School

Sale

TRIGGERED AN "ENHANCED SENTENCE" EVEN THOUGH SCHOOL WAS OUT AT THE TIME.

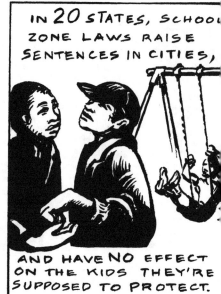

IN 20 STATES, SCHOOL ZONE LAWS RAISE SENTENCES IN CITIES,

AND HAVE NO EFFECT ON THE KIDS THEY'RE SUPPOSED TO PROTECT.

YVONNE GOT A 2 YEAR SENTENCE AND GAVE BIRTH IN SHACKLES.

SINCE NONE OF HER RELATIVES COULD HELP...

SHE HAD TO PUT HER BABY IN FOSTER CARE.

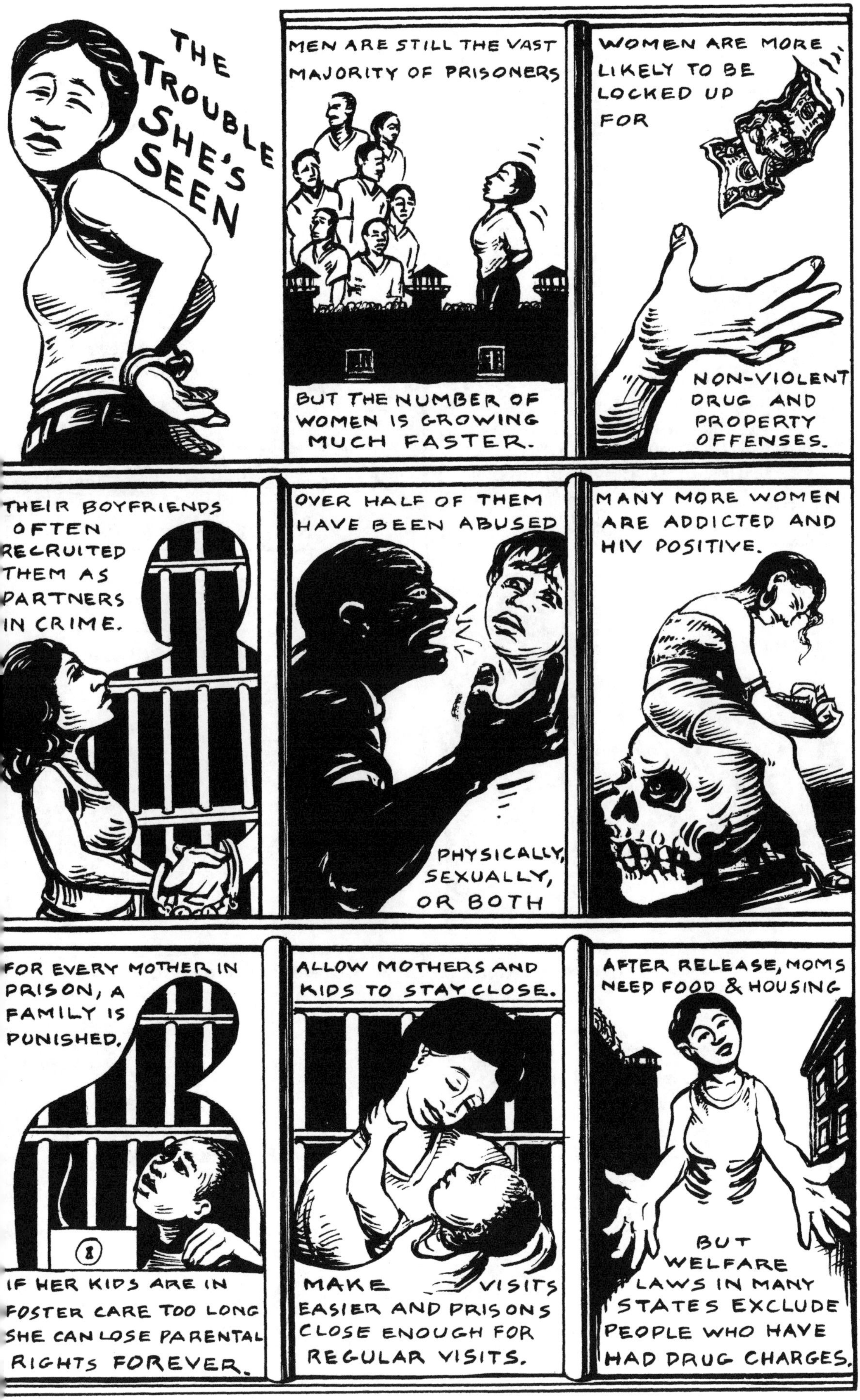
THE TROUBLE SHE'S SEEN
MEN ARE STILL THE VAST MAJORITY OF PRISONERS
BUT THE NUMBER OF WOMEN IS GROWING MUCH FASTER.
WOMEN ARE MORE LIKELY TO BE LOCKED UP FOR
NON-VIOLENT DRUG AND PROPERTY OFFENSES.
THEIR BOYFRIENDS OFTEN RECRUITED THEM AS PARTNERS IN CRIME.
OVER HALF OF THEM HAVE BEEN ABUSED
PHYSICALLY, SEXUALLY, OR BOTH
MANY MORE WOMEN ARE ADDICTED AND HIV POSITIVE.
FOR EVERY MOTHER IN PRISON, A FAMILY IS PUNISHED.
IF HER KIDS ARE IN FOSTER CARE TOO LONG SHE CAN LOSE PARENTAL RIGHTS FOREVER.
ALLOW MOTHERS AND KIDS TO STAY CLOSE.
MAKE VISITS EASIER AND PRISONS CLOSE ENOUGH FOR REGULAR VISITS.
AFTER RELEASE, MOMS NEED FOOD & HOUSING
BUT WELFARE LAWS IN MANY STATES EXCLUDE PEOPLE WHO HAVE HAD DRUG CHARGES.

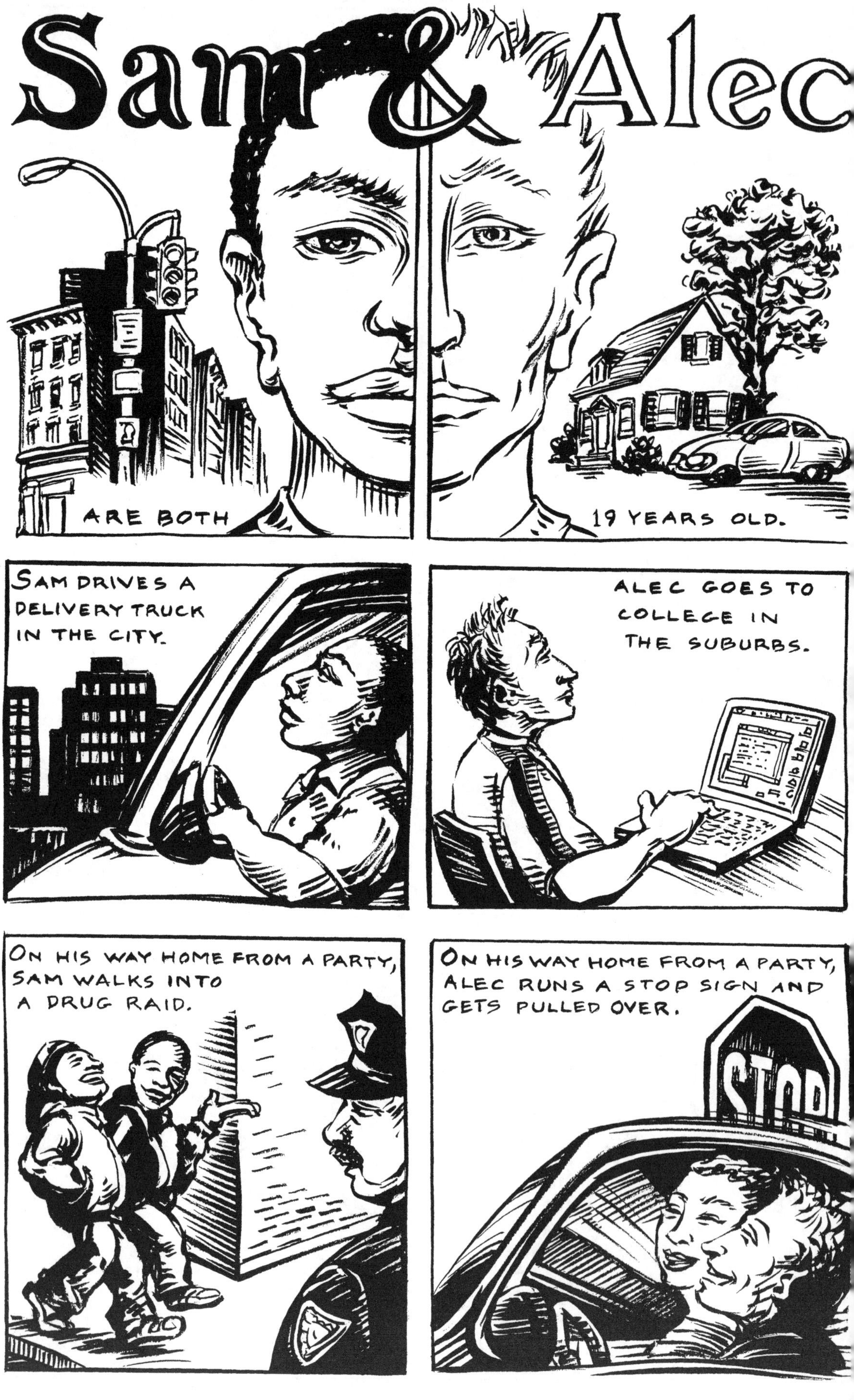
Sam & Alec
ARE BOTH
19 YEARS OLD.
SAM DRIVES A DELIVERY TRUCK IN THE CITY.
ALEC GOES TO COLLEGE IN THE SUBURBS.
ON HIS WAY HOME FROM A PARTY, SAM WALKS INTO A DRUG RAID.
ON HIS WAY HOME FROM A PARTY, ALEC RUNS A STOP SIGN AND GETS PULLED OVER.
STOP

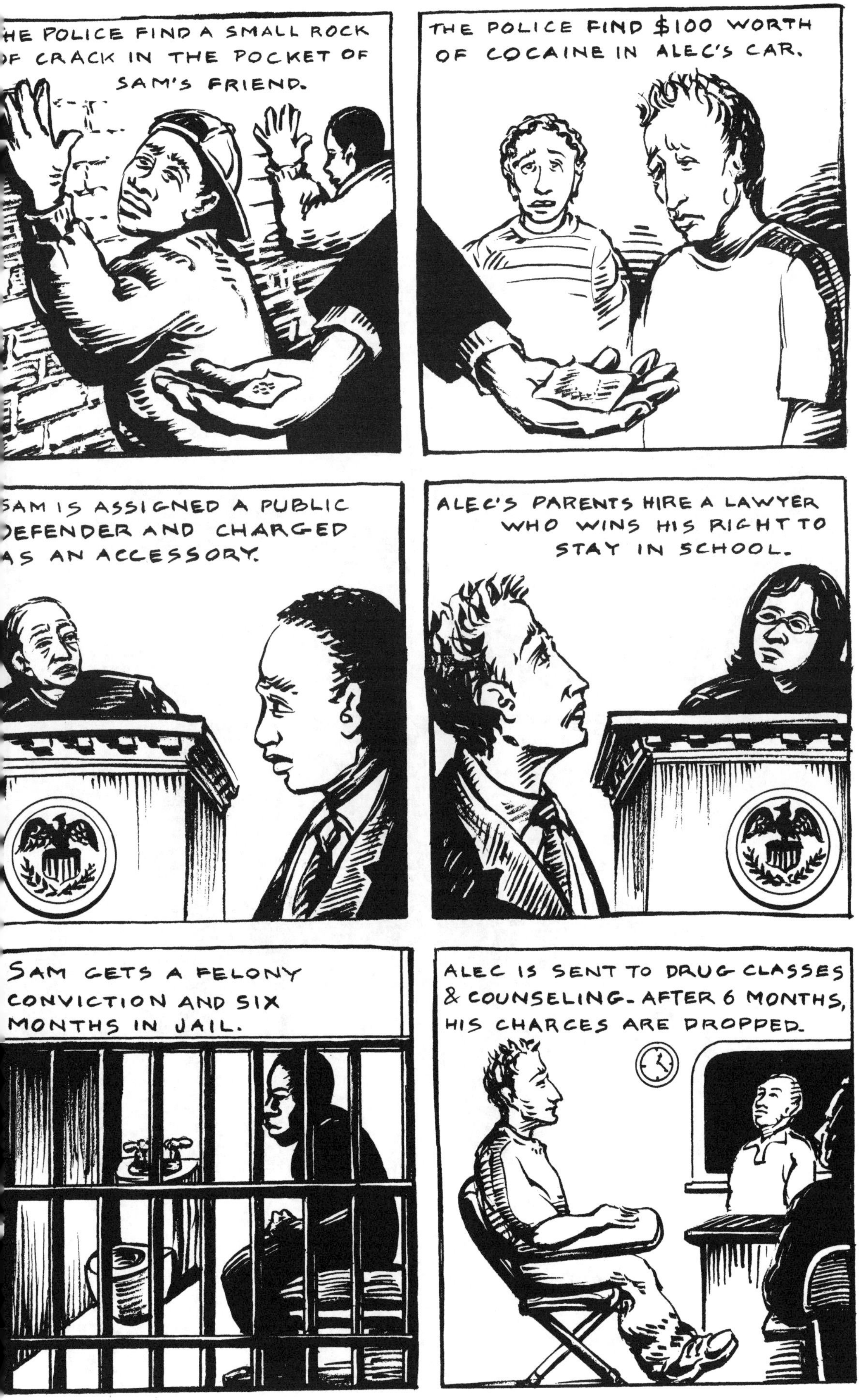
HE POLICE FIND A SMALL ROCK
F CRACK IN THE POCKET OF
SAM'S FRIEND.
THE POLICE FIND $100 WORTH
OF COCAINE IN ALEC'S CAR.
SAM IS ASSIGNED A PUBLIC
EFENDER AND CHARGED
S AN ACCESSORY.
ALEC'S PARENTS HIRE A LAWYER
WHO WINS HIS RIGHT TO
STAY IN SCHOOL.
SAM GETS A FELONY
CONVICTION AND SIX
MONTHS IN JAIL.
ALEC IS SENT TO DRUG CLASSES
& COUNSELING. AFTER 6 MONTHS,
HIS CHARGES ARE DROPPED.

WHAT'S RACE GOT TO DO WITH IT?

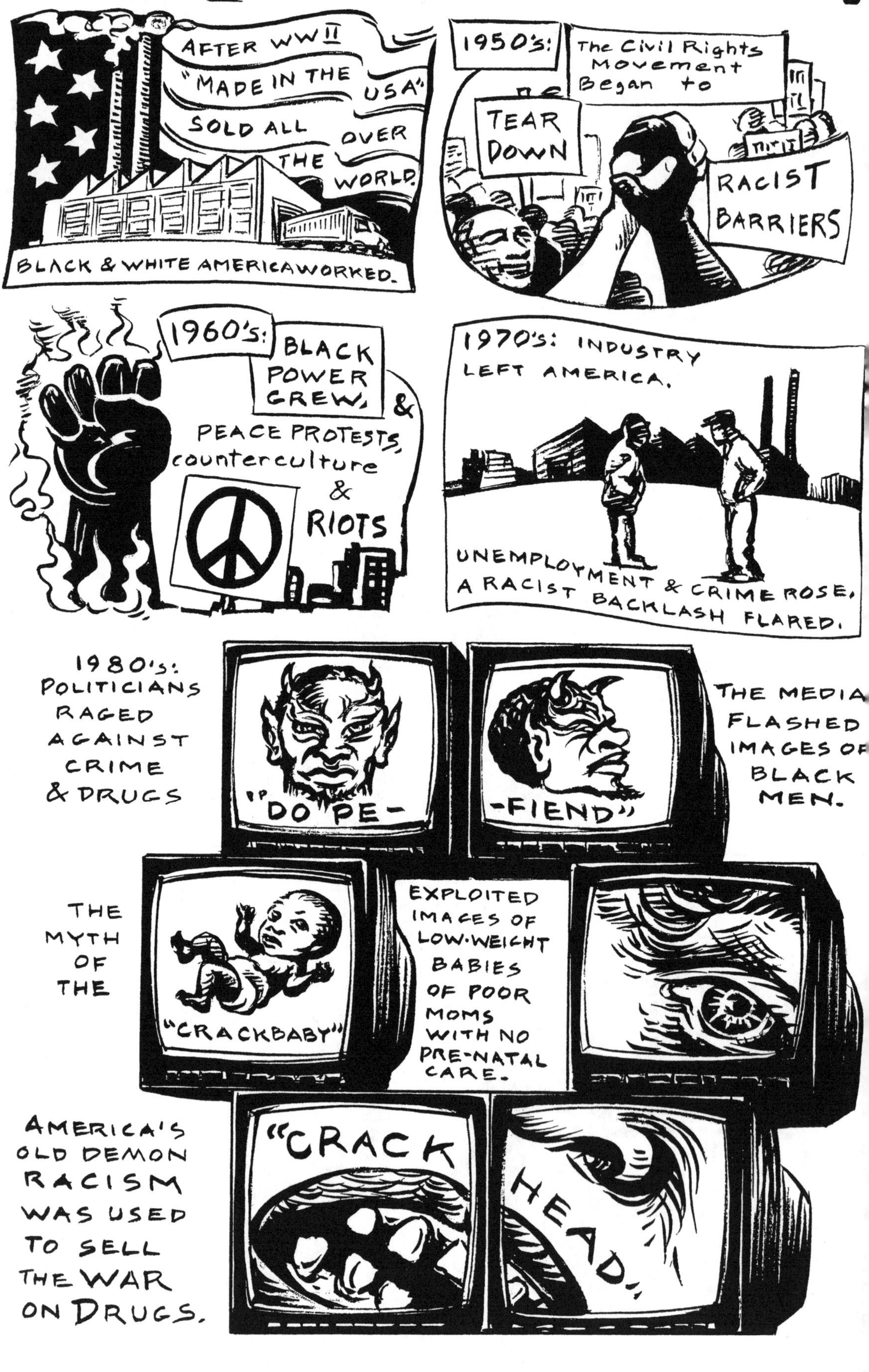

AFTER WW II "MADE IN THE USA" SOLD ALL OVER THE WORLD.
BLACK & WHITE AMERICA WORKED.
1950's:
The Civil Rights Movement Began to
TEAR DOWN
RACIST BARRIERS
1960's:
BLACK POWER GREW,
& PEACE PROTESTS, counterculture & RIOTS
1970's: INDUSTRY LEFT AMERICA.
UNEMPLOYMENT & CRIME ROSE, A RACIST BACKLASH FLARED.
1980's: POLITICIANS RAGED AGAINST CRIME & DRUGS
"DO PE-
-FIEND"
THE MEDIA FLASHED IMAGES OF BLACK MEN.
THE MYTH OF THE
"CRACKBABY"
EXPLOITED IMAGES OF LOW-WEIGHT BABIES OF POOR MOMS WITH NO PRE-NATAL CARE.
AMERICA'S OLD DEMON RACISM WAS USED TO SELL THE WAR ON DRUGS.
"CRACK
HEAD"

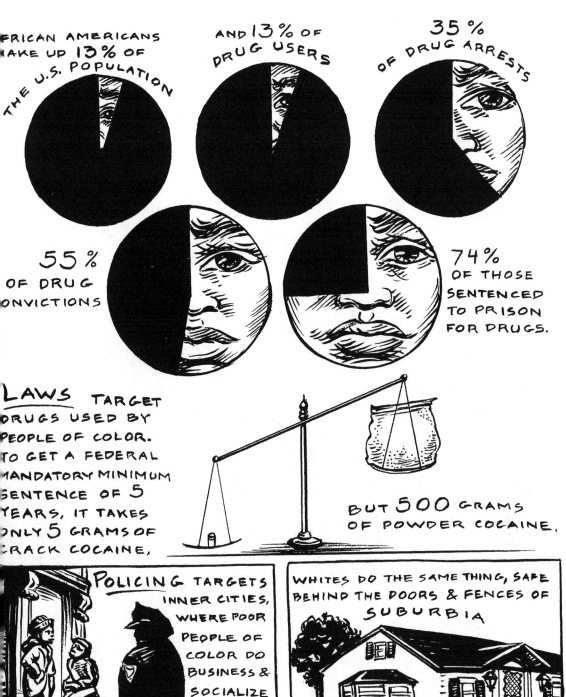

AFRICAN AMERICANS MAKE UP 13% OF THE U.S. POPULATION

AND 13% OF DRUG USERS

35% OF DRUG ARRESTS

55% OF DRUG CONVICTIONS

74% OF THOSE SENTENCED TO PRISON FOR DRUGS.

LAWS TARGET DRUGS USED BY PEOPLE OF COLOR. TO GET A FEDERAL MANDATORY MINIMUM SENTENCE OF 5 YEARS, IT TAKES ONLY 5 GRAMS OF CRACK COCAINE,

BUT 500 GRAMS OF POWDER COCAINE.

POLICING TARGETS INNER CITIES, WHERE POOR PEOPLE OF COLOR DO BUSINESS & SOCIALIZE OUT ON THE STREET.

WHITES DO THE SAME THING, SAFE BEHIND THE DOORS & FENCES OF SUBURBIA

ONCE THEY'RE CAUGHT, AFRICAN-AMERICANS ARE MORE LIKELY TO GET PRISON TIME.

WHITES ARE MORE LIKELY TO GET ACCESS TO TREATMENT.

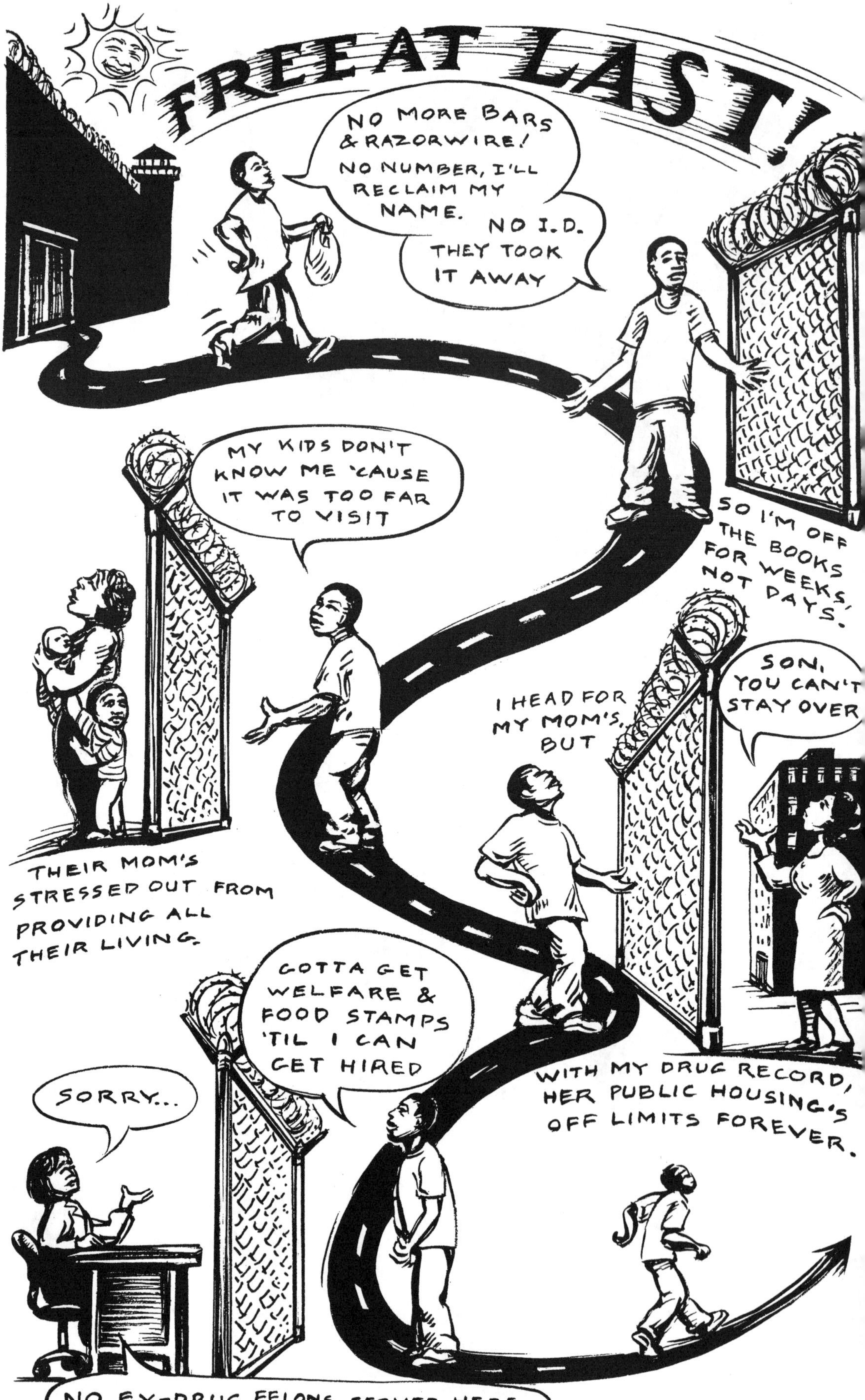

FREE AT LAST!
NO MORE BARS & RAZORWIRE! NO NUMBER, I'LL RECLAIM MY NAME.
NO I.D. THEY TOOK IT AWAY
SO I'M OFF THE BOOKS FOR WEEKS, NOT DAYS.
MY KIDS DON'T KNOW ME 'CAUSE IT WAS TOO FAR TO VISIT
THEIR MOM'S STRESSED OUT FROM PROVIDING ALL THEIR LIVING.
I HEAD FOR MY MOM'S, BUT
SON, YOU CAN'T STAY OVER
WITH MY DRUG RECORD, HER PUBLIC HOUSING'S OFF LIMITS FOREVER.
GOTTA GET WELFARE & FOOD STAMPS 'TIL I CAN GET HIRED
SORRY...
NO EX-DRUG FELONS SERVED HERE.

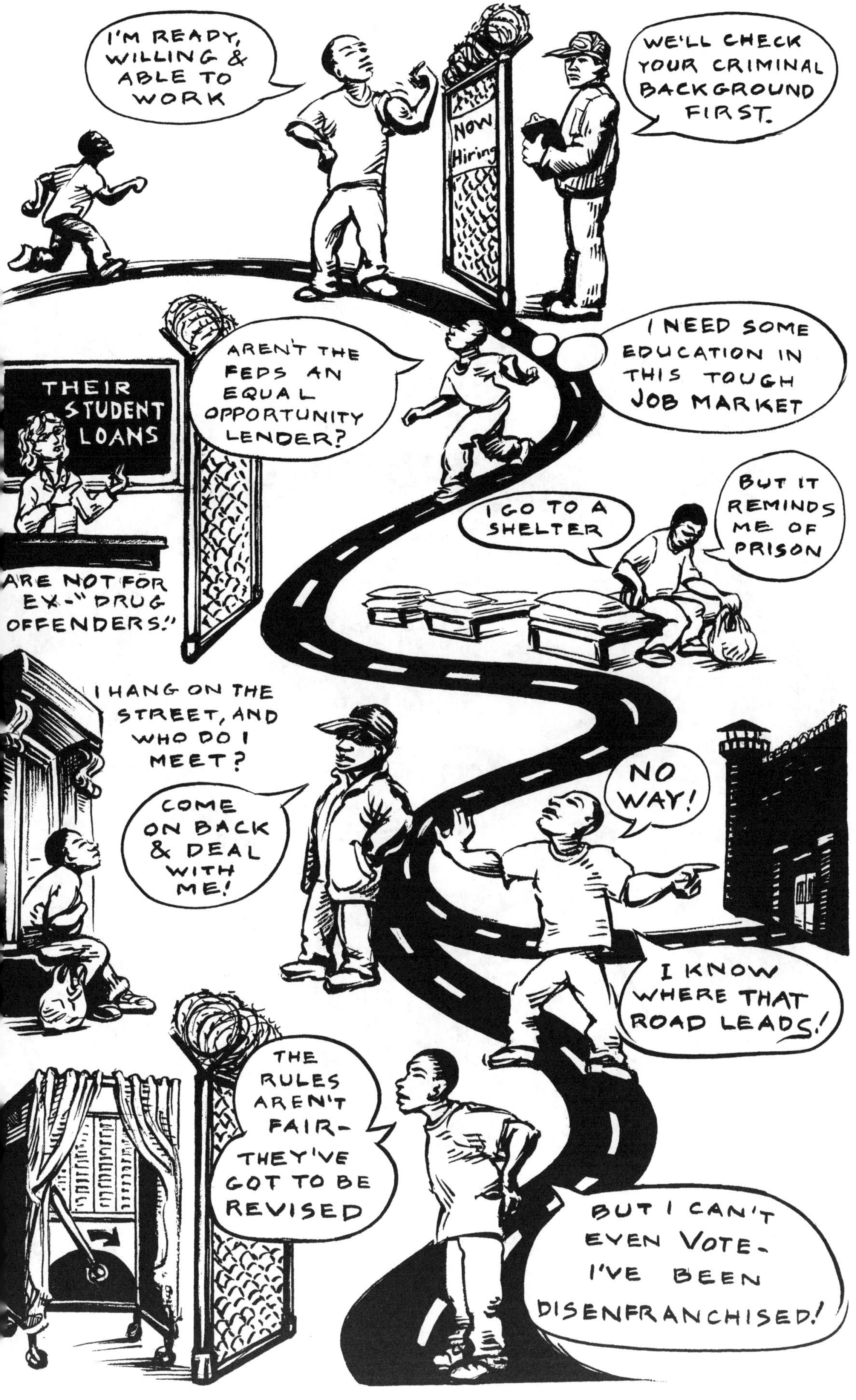
I'M READY, WILLING & ABLE TO WORK
WE'LL CHECK YOUR CRIMINAL BACKGROUND FIRST.
Now Hiring
I NEED SOME EDUCATION IN THIS TOUGH JOB MARKET
AREN'T THE FEDS AN EQUAL OPPORTUNITY LENDER?
THEIR STUDENT LOANS
ARE NOT FOR EX-"DRUG OFFENDERS."
I GO TO A SHELTER
BUT IT REMINDS ME OF PRISON
I HANG ON THE STREET, AND WHO DO I MEET?
COME ON BACK & DEAL WITH ME!
NO WAY!
I KNOW WHERE THAT ROAD LEADS!
THE RULES AREN'T FAIR- THEY'VE GOT TO BE REVISED
BUT I CAN'T EVEN VOTE- I'VE BEEN DISENFRANCHISED!

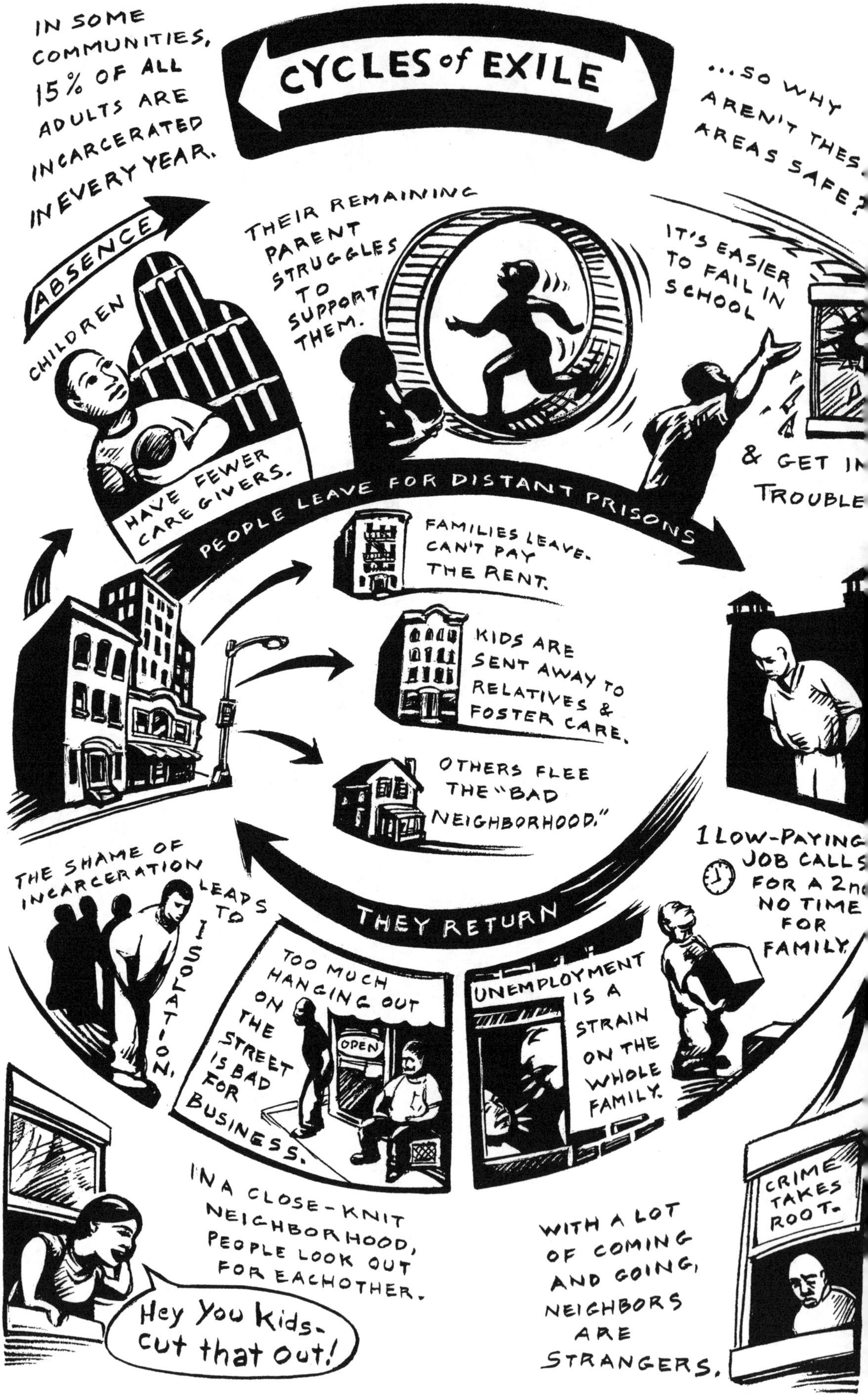
CYCLES of EXILE
IN SOME COMMUNITIES, 15% OF ALL ADULTS ARE INCARCERATED IN EVERY YEAR.
...SO WHY AREN'T THES AREAS SAFE?
ABSENCE
CHILDREN HAVE FEWER CARE GIVERS.
THEIR REMAINING PARENT STRUGGLES TO SUPPORT THEM.
IT'S EASIER TO FAIL IN SCHOOL
& GET IN TROUBLE
PEOPLE LEAVE FOR DISTANT PRISONS
FAMILIES LEAVE. CAN'T PAY THE RENT.
KIDS ARE SENT AWAY TO RELATIVES & FOSTER CARE.
OTHERS FLEE THE "BAD NEIGHBORHOOD."
1 LOW-PAYING JOB CALLS FOR A 2n NO TIME FOR FAMILY.
THEY RETURN
THE SHAME OF INCARCERATION LEADS TO ISOLATION.
TOO MUCH HANGING OUT ON THE STREET IS BAD FOR BUSINESS.
OPEN
UNEMPLOYMENT IS A STRAIN ON THE WHOLE FAMILY.
IN A CLOSE-KNIT NEIGHBORHOOD, PEOPLE LOOK OUT FOR EACHOTHER.
Hey You kids-cut that out!
WITH A LOT OF COMING AND GOING, NEIGHBORS ARE STRANGERS.
CRIME TAKES ROOT.

These ideas are based on the work of Dina R. Rose and Todd R. Clear: "Incarceration, Reentry and Social Capital: Social Networks in the Balance,

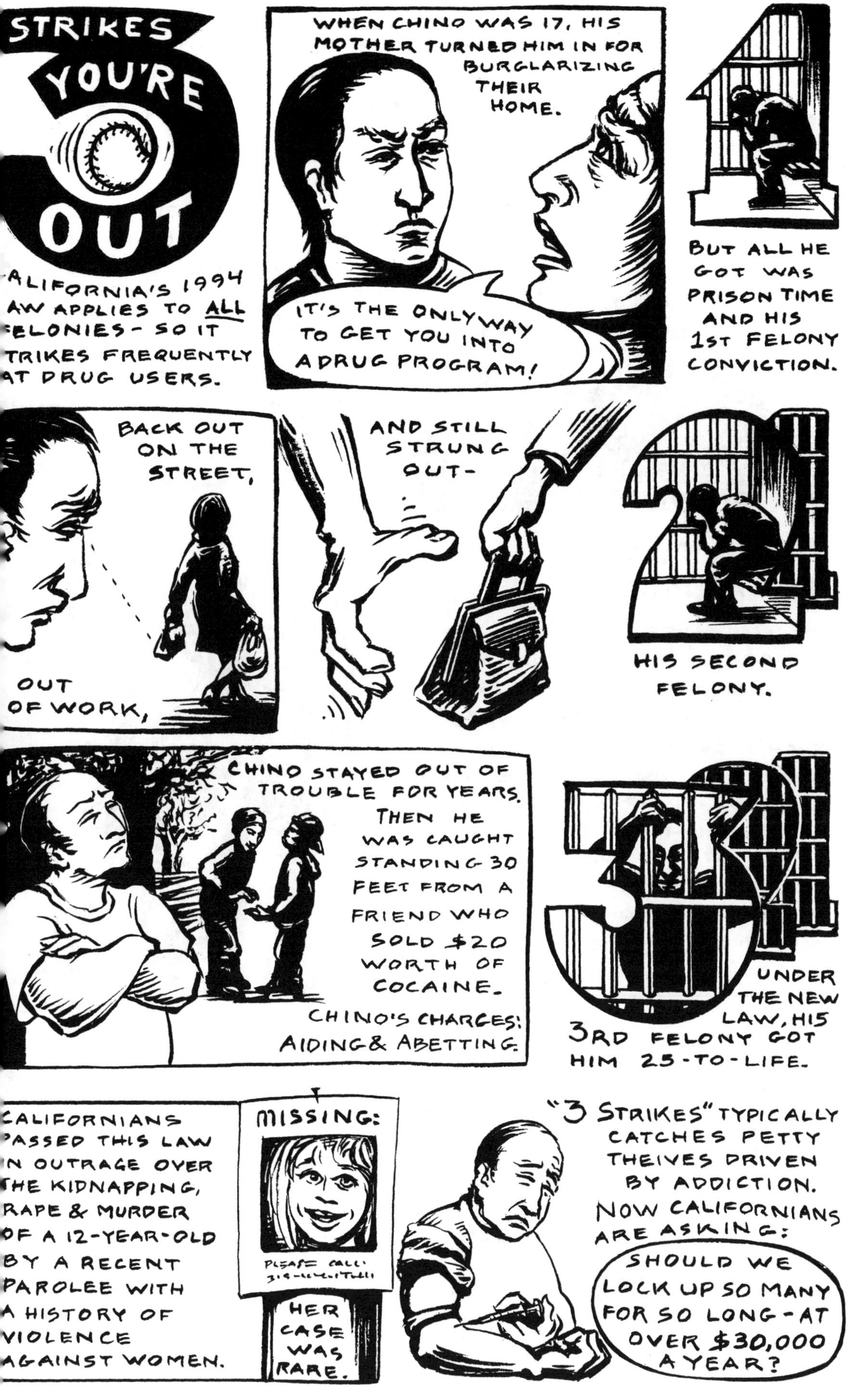

STRIKES
YOU'RE
OUT
ALIFORNIA'S 1994 AW APPLIES TO ALL ELONIES - SO IT TRIKES FREQUENTLY AT DRUG USERS.
WHEN CHINO WAS 17, HIS MOTHER TURNED HIM IN FOR BURGLARIZING THEIR HOME.
IT'S THE ONLY WAY TO GET YOU INTO A DRUG PROGRAM!
BUT ALL HE GOT WAS PRISON TIME AND HIS 1st FELONY CONVICTION.
BACK OUT ON THE STREET,
OUT OF WORK,
AND STILL STRUNG OUT-
HIS SECOND FELONY.
CHINO STAYED OUT OF TROUBLE FOR YEARS. THEN HE WAS CAUGHT STANDING 30 FEET FROM A FRIEND WHO SOLD $20 WORTH OF COCAINE.
CHINO'S CHARGES: AIDING & ABETTING.
UNDER THE NEW LAW, HIS 3RD FELONY GOT HIM 25-TO-LIFE.
ALIFORNIANS ASSED THIS LAW N OUTRAGE OVER HE KIDNAPPING, RAPE & MURDER OF A 12-YEAR-OLD BY A RECENT PAROLEE WITH A HISTORY OF VIOLENCE AGAINST WOMEN.
MISSING:
HER CASE WAS RARE.
"3 STRIKES" TYPICALLY CATCHES PETTY THEIVES DRIVEN BY ADDICTION. NOW CALIFORNIANS ARE ASKING:
SHOULD WE LOCK UP SO MANY FOR SO LONG - AT OVER $30,000 A YEAR?

THE WAR ON DRUGS HAS COST TAXPAYERS BILLIONS, DEVASTATED LIVES, FAMILIES & COMMUNITIES AND COMPLETELY FAILED TO REDUCE DRUG USE.

CONSIDER THESE ALTERNATIVES

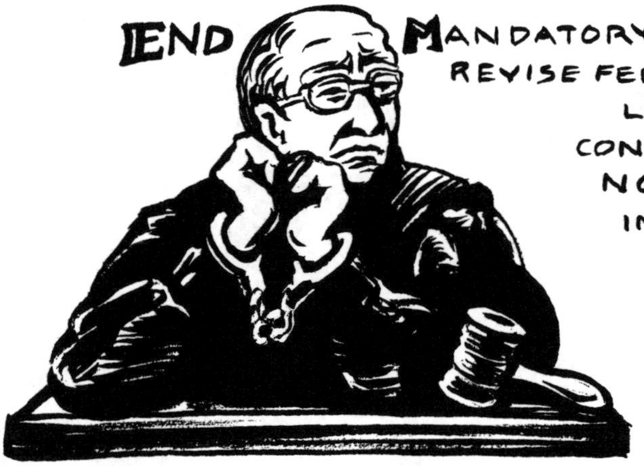

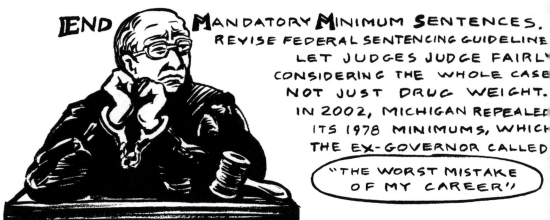

END MANDATORY MINIMUM SENTENCES.

REVISE FEDERAL SENTENCING GUIDELINE LET JUDGES JUDGE FAIRL CONSIDERING THE WHOLE CASE NOT JUST DRUG WEIGHT. IN 2002, MICHIGAN REPEALED ITS 1978 MINIMUMS, WHICH THE EX-GOVERNOR CALLED

"THE WORST MISTAKE OF MY CAREER"

OFFER DRUG TREATMENT

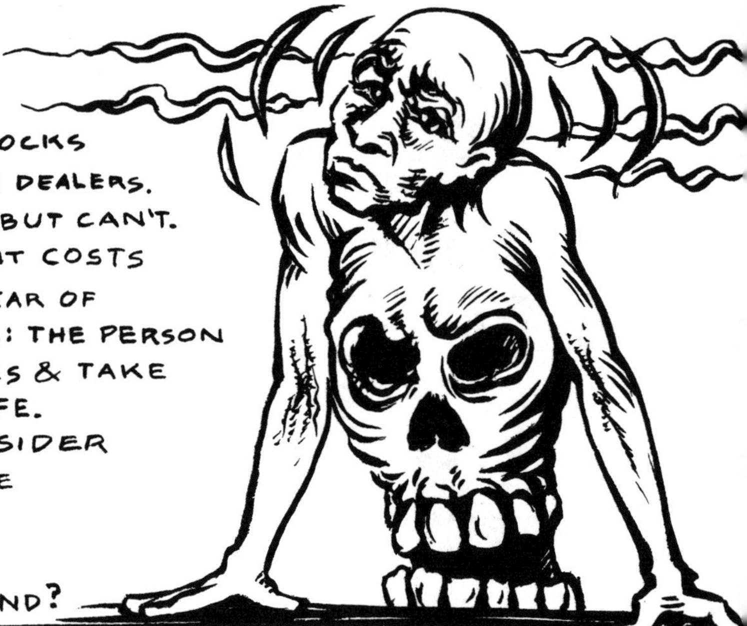

THE WAR ON DRUGS LOCKS UP MORE USERS THAN DEALERS. MOST WANT TO QUIT, BUT CAN'T. A YEAR OF TREATMENT COSTS MUCH LESS THAN A YEAR OF INCARCERATION, PLUS: THE PERSON CAN WORK, PAY TAXES & TAKE PART IN FAMILY LIFE. A FEW STATES CONSIDER TREATMENT BEFORE INCARCERATION. WHY NOT OFFER TREATMENT ON DEMAND?

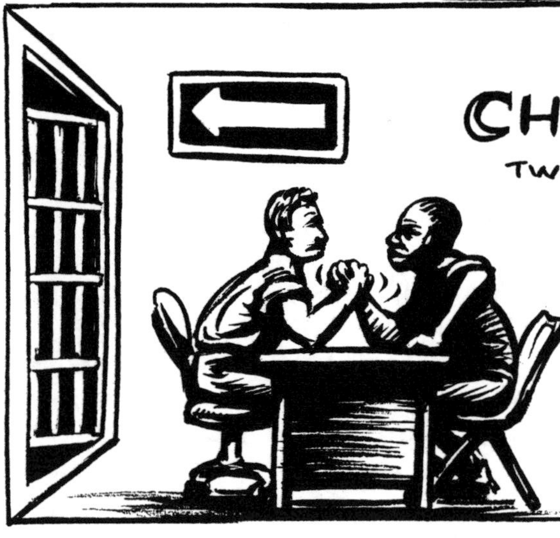

CHANGE PROBATION

TWO THIRDS OF PEOPLE ON PROBATION ARE RE-ARRESTED, MOSTLY ON TECHNICAL VIOLATIONS, LIKE MISSED APPOINTMENTS AND FAILED DRUG TESTS, NOT NEW CRIMES.

PROBATION OFFICERS SHOUL HAVE RESOURCES TO HEL PEOPLE STAY OUT OF PRISON.

END LEGAL DISCRIMINATION

AGAINST PEOPLE WHO HAVE ONE THEIR TIME. LET THEM LEAVE PRISON BEHIND. RESTORE FULL ACCESS TO PUBLIC HOUSING, WELFARE, FOOD STAMPS, STUDENT FINANCIAL AID, DRIVERS' LICENCES, STATE LICENSED PROFESSIONS & VOTING RIGHTS.

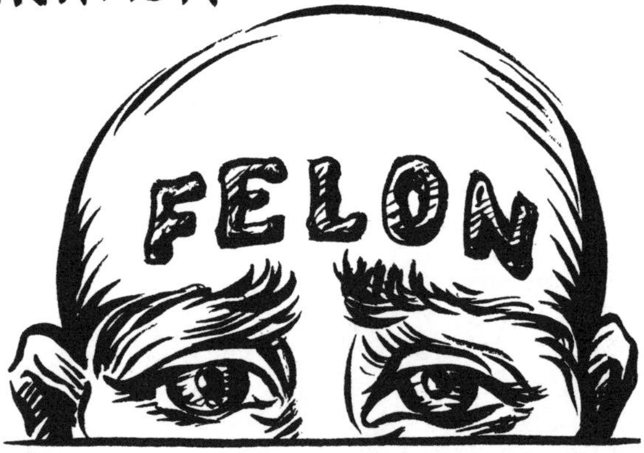
FELON

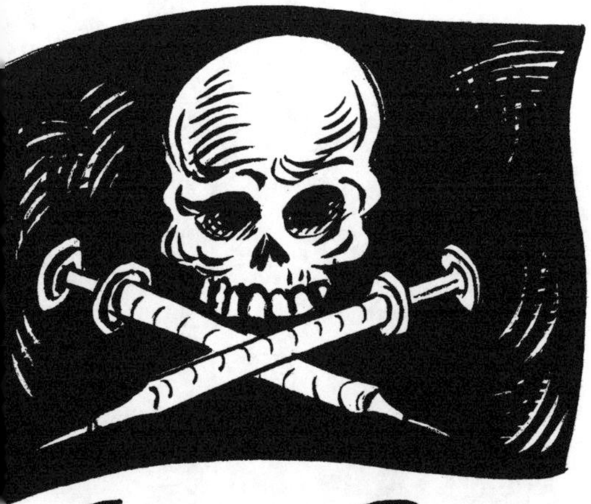

HARM REDUCTION

REDUCE THE HARMFUL EFFECTS OF DRUG USE ON FAMILIES, COMMUNITIES & THE DRUG USER. NEEDLE EXCHANGE PROGRAMS REDUCE TRANSMISSION OF HIV & HEPATITIS C.

JUSTICE REINVESTMENT

CREATE SAFER, VIABLE COMMUNITIES BY LETTING THE PEOPLE WHO LIVE THERE TAKE CONTROL OF THE MONEY SPENT ON

POLICE
PRISONS
JAILS &
COURTS,

AND INVEST IT IN:

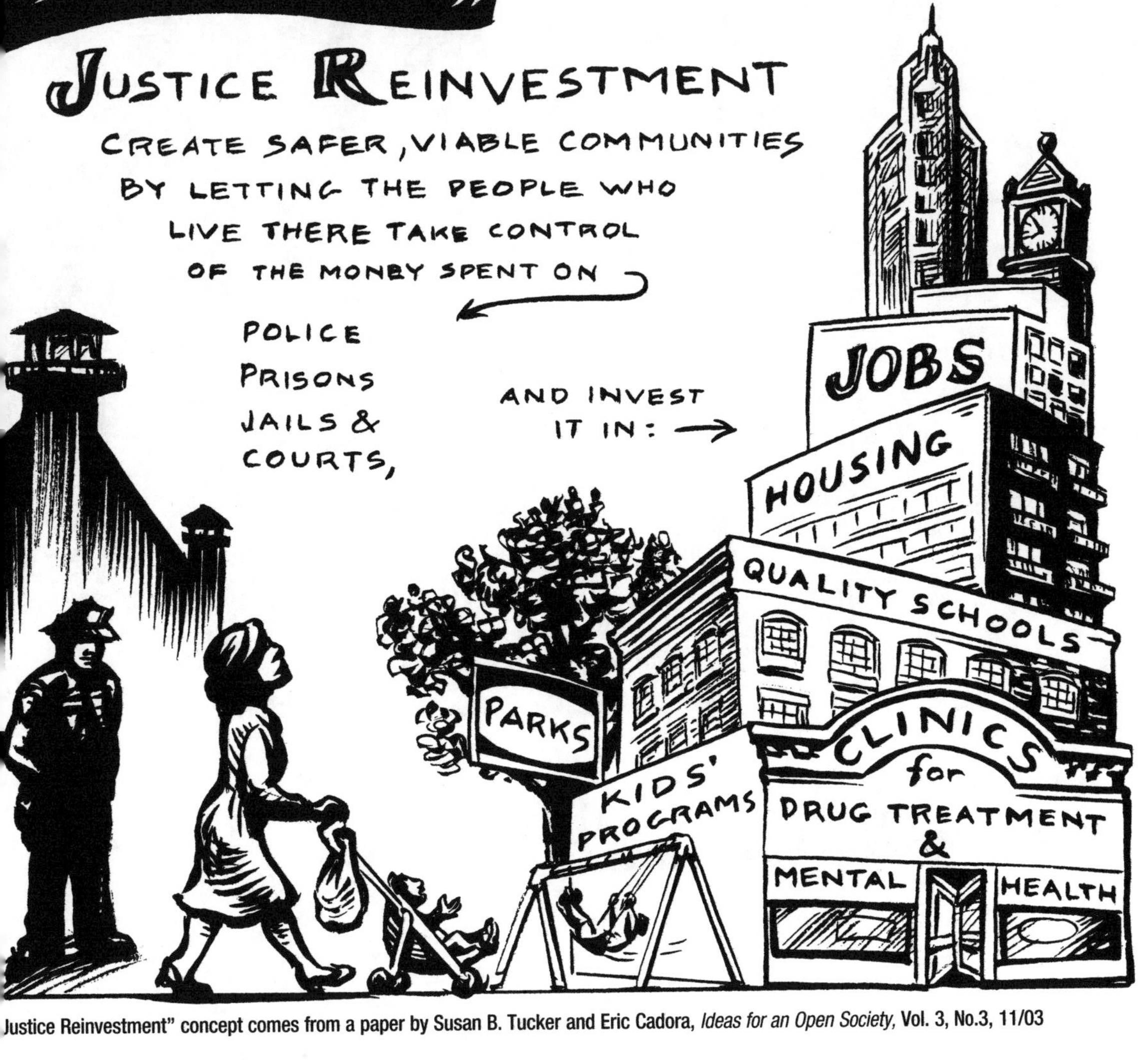
JOBS
HOUSING
QUALITY SCHOOLS
PARKS
KIDS' PROGRAMS
CLINICS for DRUG TREATMENT & MENTAL HEALTH

Justice Reinvestment" concept comes from a paper by Susan B. Tucker and Eric Cadora, *Ideas for an Open Society,* Vol. 3, No.3, 11/03

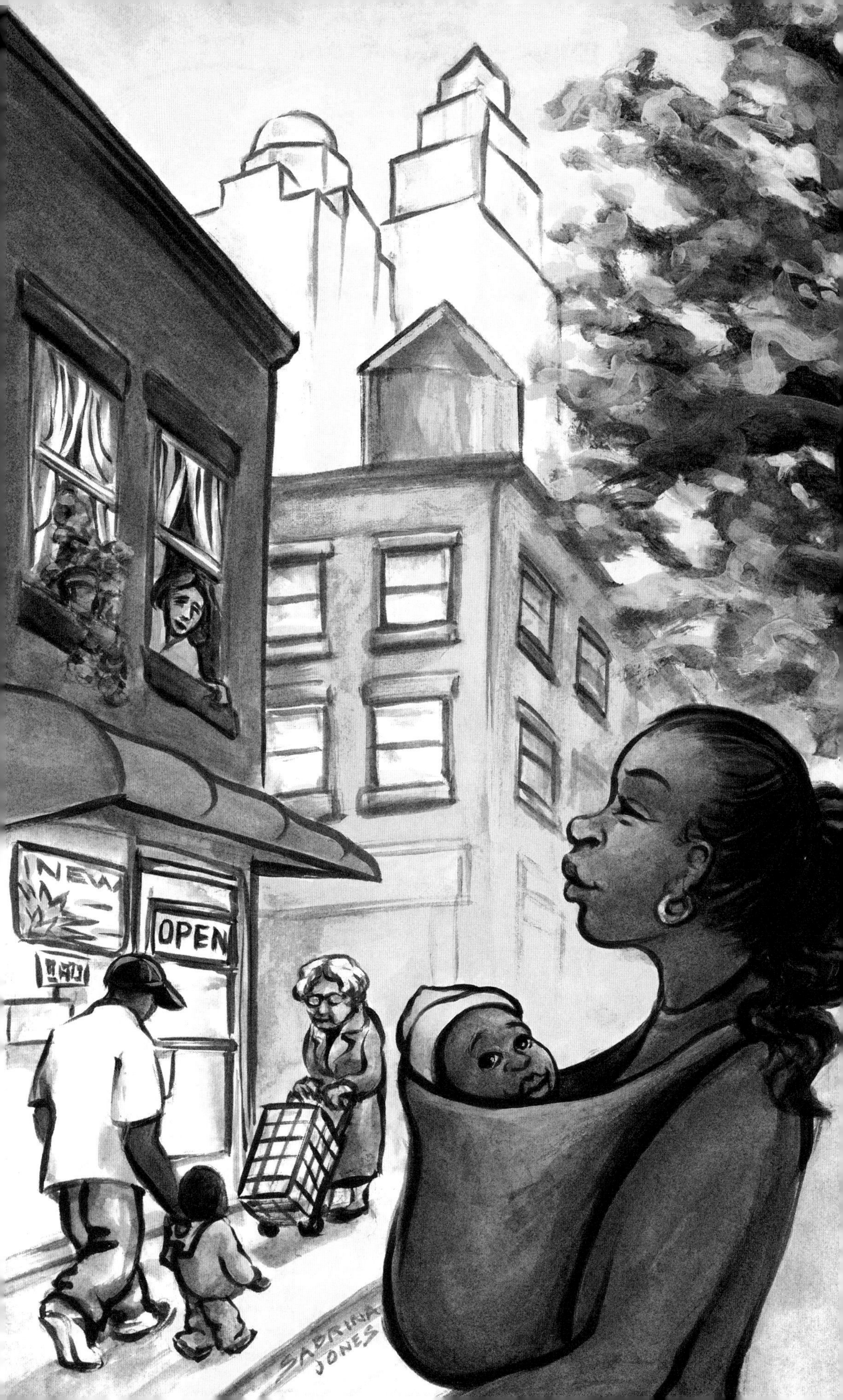
NEW
OPEN
SABRINA JONES

readers respond

As a young Hispanic woman I felt that I could relate to many of the characters in the comics. Discriminated against by class, age and gender, these women often have no place to turn. One simple mistake can ruin the rest of their lives, tear apart their families and cause permanent punishments. Facts like "93% of all people incarcerated in NY with drug offences are African American or Hispanic" epitomize the racism that is embedded in our society, no matter how much our state takes pride in being fair and a melting pot of people of all cultures. You don't have to look far to find racism, and the treatment of prisoners is a perfect example of this.

–MICHELLE BURSCHTIN
Feminist Theory Class
NYC Lab High School

I have been moved to a new facility and unfortunately during the inventory of my property, the comic books you sent me were either confiscated or lost. Would you please send me another set? They sparked a lot of conversation not only with the other prisoners but staff that that I shared them with as well.

–TERRY OLNEY
Omaha, NE

The comic books from the Real Cost of Prison Project are the easiest to read by far of any information in circulation about the criminal justice system and its impact on communities and families. As a lecturer at CUNY, I have found the comic books to be a vital source of information for students who do not understand the complexities and impacts of the criminal justice system in New York. After reading *Prisoners of the War on Drugs* one student stated, "I had no idea that pregnant women were shackled to their gurneys while giving birth. In the case of substance-abusing birthing women, the punishment definitely outweighs the crime."

–TINA REYNOLDS, MSW
Women on the Rise Telling HerStory
(WORTH)
New York, NY

The Real Cost of Prisons comic books are a seminal combination of statistics with the arresting personification of a graphic-novel format, presenting readers with a shockingly new and insightful perspective on what they assumed they knew about the criminal justice system in the United States.

–JON MARC TAYLOR, PhD.
Author
The Prisoners' Guerilla Handbook to Corre-
spondence Programs in the United States.
Crossroads Correctional Center, MO

Because of The Real Cost of Prisons comic books, small towns like mine are able to start 2008 without the whir of bulldozers making way for a prison in the middle of our community under the false pretense of economic development. I am quite sure that the subject will come up again in the future of our community, but we have fought the project off and have learned lots.

–TASHA GREENE
Co-Founder
Citizens Against the Ault Prison
Ault, Colorado

My name is Marlon Altan and I am a social studies teacher with 5 Keys Charter School. 5 Keys charter school is a high school that works out of the San Francisco County Jail. We are the first charter high school to work out of a county jail. We work with both incarcerated men and women from the ages of 18 to 60+. It is called 5 Keys because the founders thought that there were or are 5 keys to lowering the recidivism rate and those are family, recovery, education, employment and community. Currently I'm teaching economics and have found a serious disconnect between standard economics teaching material and the population that we are supposed to be serving. I've recently been exposed to your work and I think it is really amazing what you've done with the comic book. Since first reading it, I've felt it pressing to structure curriculum around the realities of the prison industrial complex. I plan on having students apply a benefit/cost analysis to the prison system and simulate a city council meeting in which students represent various interest groups and argue for or against the building of a new prison in a town. I also plan on having the students research the real cost of county jail in San Francisco. The comic book on women and prison could be a vital resource specific to the incarcerated women in San Francisco. I could see it empowering the women to take control of their lives and start working for positive change. Every 5 weeks I have a new class of up to 45 students.

–MARLON ALTAN
5 Keys Charter School
San Francisco, CA

A grand example of written language and cartoon art being used to educate, inform and hopefully inspire young folks to turn away from anti-social and self-destructive behavior that feeds the prison-industrial-complex. There cannot be a prison-building moratorium or abolition movement without a voice advocating in such a way that reaches those most impacted by the system of incarceration. These comic books are that voice and an important contribution to that movement.

–JALIL A. MUNTAQIM
Political prisoner

This collection of comic books is an important, accessible resource for human rights, prisoners' rights, and community activists. The comics deal with fundamental realities and the most basic issues clearly and respectfully.

–MARA TAUB
Coordinator
Coalition for Prisoners' Rights
Santa Fe, NM

An excellent tool and catalyst to create consciousness among the misinformed, this book will help people see prisoners, and the cost associated, as they truly are. There exists a huge impediment in our society. People prefer to think about almost anything so long as it does not involve thinking about prison and prisoners.

Rather than alleviate prison overpopulation by reviewing cases and releasing those who deserve it, the system builds more prisons. Do we ever stop to ask ourselves what the real cost is? What is the mentality or philosophy driving this? The reality is that the prison system has become a very lucrative industry. It is the only major industry in America that still has future growth and profit potential.

What mechanisms are in place to help alleviate this grotesque problem? One thing we can do is to create awareness and provide truth. This is exactly what the comic books accomplish.

–LUIS GONZALEZ AND JOSE FELIX
California State Prison
Corcoran, CA

An amazing resource that all educators need to read and use. I used *Prison Town* as a teaching resource in my Economics classes to show how our tax money is used to perpetuate the racial inequities that exist in our society. It worked wonderfully.

–DAN LE
Social Science Teacher
Fremont High School
Los Angeles, CA

For over two years, RIHD has presented copies of all three comic books to at-risk youth, prisoners, ex-prisoners & their families, legislators and concerned citizens. We can't keep up with the requests for copies.

The Virginia Department of Corrections hands out "prisoner manuals" and RIHD hands out RCPP books to assist prisoners with their rehabilitation through education & knowledge. They have "healed" many prisoners through education and facts!

–LILLIE (MS. K) BRANCH-KENNEDY
Executive Director
Resource Information Help for the
Disadvantaged, R.I.H.D., Inc.
Richmond, VA

As a long-time volunteer in a medium-security prison and a volunteer with Wisconsin Books to Prisoners, I've distributed hundreds of these comics to prisoners, their families, students, and other "free" people. I can attest to the value these comics have as a tool to spark public awareness about the American gulag. People who have admitted their ignorance—-even their indifference—-to the destructiveness of mass incarceration have been moved and outraged by the information presented in these comics. In a cruel and violent society, outrage is extremely important to cultivate; (we radicals know) this emotion has always been a critical precursor to social change.

–CAMY MATTHAY
Wisconsin Books to Prisoners

Here in the central valley, also known as "Prison Alley," it's crucial that we get as much information out as possible on the cost of prisons in our communities to our communities. Because the valley is poverty-stricken, it is vital that we counter the idea that prisons bring in jobs and economic windfalls.

I have found that people pick up these books while waiting in line and to take them home to their kids. If possible, I would take a case to every middle and high school in the valley.

–DEBBIE REYES
Central Valley Coordinator
California Prison Moratorium Project
Fresno, CA

Vermont has seen a dramatic increase in incarceration of women over the last decade, the vast majority of whom are survivors of domestic and/or sexual violence. Advocates from our local domestic and sexual violence programs lead domestic violence educational support groups in the women's prisons in VT and provide The Real Cost of Prisons comic books to women who attend their groups. These wonderful comics are accessible, engaging, beautiful and profound, offering women opportunities to feel connected with other women across the country, to make connections between tragedies in their own lives and larger injustices in our society, and to transform the personal to the political.

–CHANI WATERHOUSE
Program Support Coordinator
VT Network Against Domestic
and Sexual Violence

There's more than one way to tell a story. And while the incarceration of so many fathers and sons, mothers and daughters, aunts and uncles, cousins and friends is no laughing matter, comic books have proven to be yet another effective method.

Though in comic book form, The Real Cost of Prisons Project illustrates the real: the societal repercussions of millions of idly caged and the release of some 600,000 mostly unprepared parolees every year across the red, white and blue.

The comics contain stories about individual impact, family detriment and community, county and state consequences. In addition, we learn how this dark industry spawned and spurred, who profits from prisons, and some of the back-door "politricks" used to get us so entrenched in failure.

Every American has a duty to question how this vast amount of taxpayer money is being spent and to investigate whether such unchecked incarceration is moral or not.

–DORTELL WILLIAMS
California State Prison
Lancaster, CA

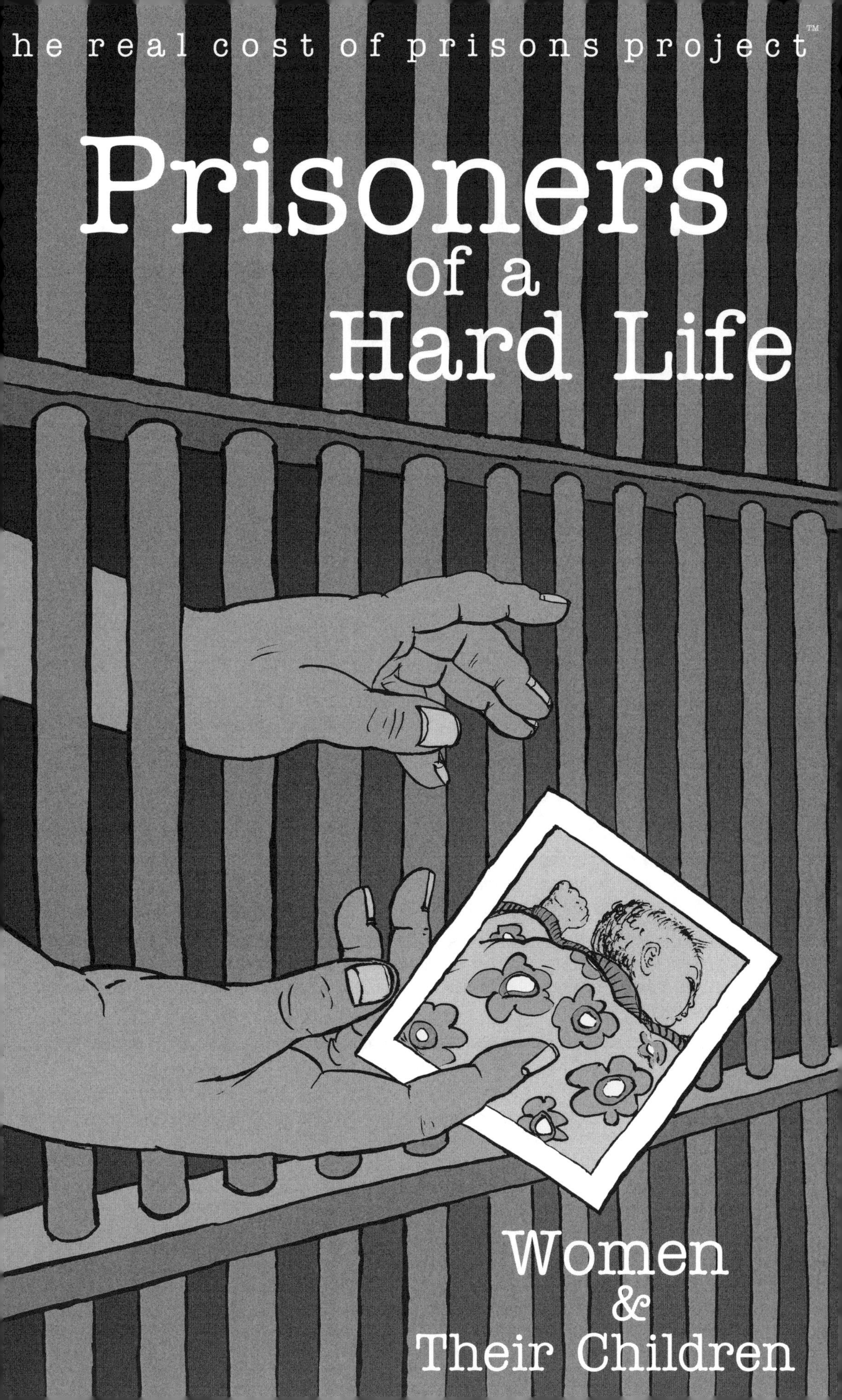
he real cost of prisons project™
Prisoners
of a
Hard Life
Women
&
Their Children

the real cost of prisons projec

www.realcostofprisons.org • info@realcostofprisons.org

Prisoners
of a Hard Life
Women & Their Children

Artist: Susan Willmarth

Writers: Ellen Miller-Mack, Susan Willmarth, Lois Ahrens

Real Cost of Prisons On Women & Their Children Workshop
writer/presenter: Kiaran Honderich

Art Direction, Design & Cover Color: Chris Shadoian

Real Cost of Prisons Project Director: Lois Ahrens

The Real Cost of Prisons Project brings together prison/justice policy activists with political economists to create workshops and materials which explore both the immediate and long-term costs of mass incarceration on the individual, her/his family, community and the nation.

Two additional comic books are part of this series: *Prison Town: Paying the Price* and *Prisoners of the War On Drugs.* If you would like copies of our comic books to assist your group in its organizing work, contact Lois Ahrens. Or you can download the entire series for free from our website: www.real-costofprisons.org.

Any reproduction requires written permission of the Real Cost of Prisons Project, except for small excerpts for review or publicity purposes. Please credit the Real Cost of Prisons Project.

The Real Cost of Prisons Project is an activity of The Sentencing Project, a Washington, DC based non-profit dedicated to reducing over-reliance on incarceration. The Real Cost of Prisons Project is supported by a grant from the Community Advocacy Project of the Open Society Institute.

THANK YOU
Dana Kaplan, Dina Rose, Todd Clear, Eric Cadora, Women's Prison Association, Lynn Paltrow and National Advocates for Pregnant Women, Families Against Mandatory Minimums, N.C. Christopher Couch, James Heinz, Mark Brenner, Marc Mauer, Malcolm Young, Raquiba LaBrie, William Johnston and Helena Huang.

And to the women whose lives and families have been disrupted by incarceration.
We are grateful for what we learn from you.

OUT OF EVERY 109 WOMEN IN AMERICA S INCARCERATED, ON PAROLE OR PROBATION

150,000 women are in jail or in prison[1]

MOST WOMEN ENTERING PRISON HAVE EEN CONVICTED F NON-VIOLENT CRIMES[2]		½ OF ALL WOMEN IN PRISON ARE INCARCERATED MORE THAN 100 MILES FROM THEIR FAMILIES[3]		INCARCERATED WOMEN ARE AMONG THE POOREST PEOPLE IN AMERICA. 2/3 HAVE LESS THAN A HIGH SCHOOL EDUCATION. ONE IN FIVE HOMELESS[4]

ALMOST ½ OF THE WOMEN ENTERING PRISON IN 2000 WERE SERVING TIME FOR DRUG OFFENCES[5]

SEVEN MILLION CHILDREN HAVE A PARENT IN PRISON, ON PROBATION OR ON PAROLE[6]

AFRICAN AMERICANS ARE 18% OF N.Y. STATE'S POPULATION[7]

HISPANICS ARE 15.1% OF N.Y. STATE'S POPULATION[8]

79% OF ALL WOMEN IN N.Y. STATE'S PRISONS ARE BLACK OR HISPANIC[9]

OF ALL PEOPLE INCARCERATED IN NEW YORK WITH DRUG OFFENCES:

93% ARE AFRICAN AMERICAN OR HISPANIC[10]

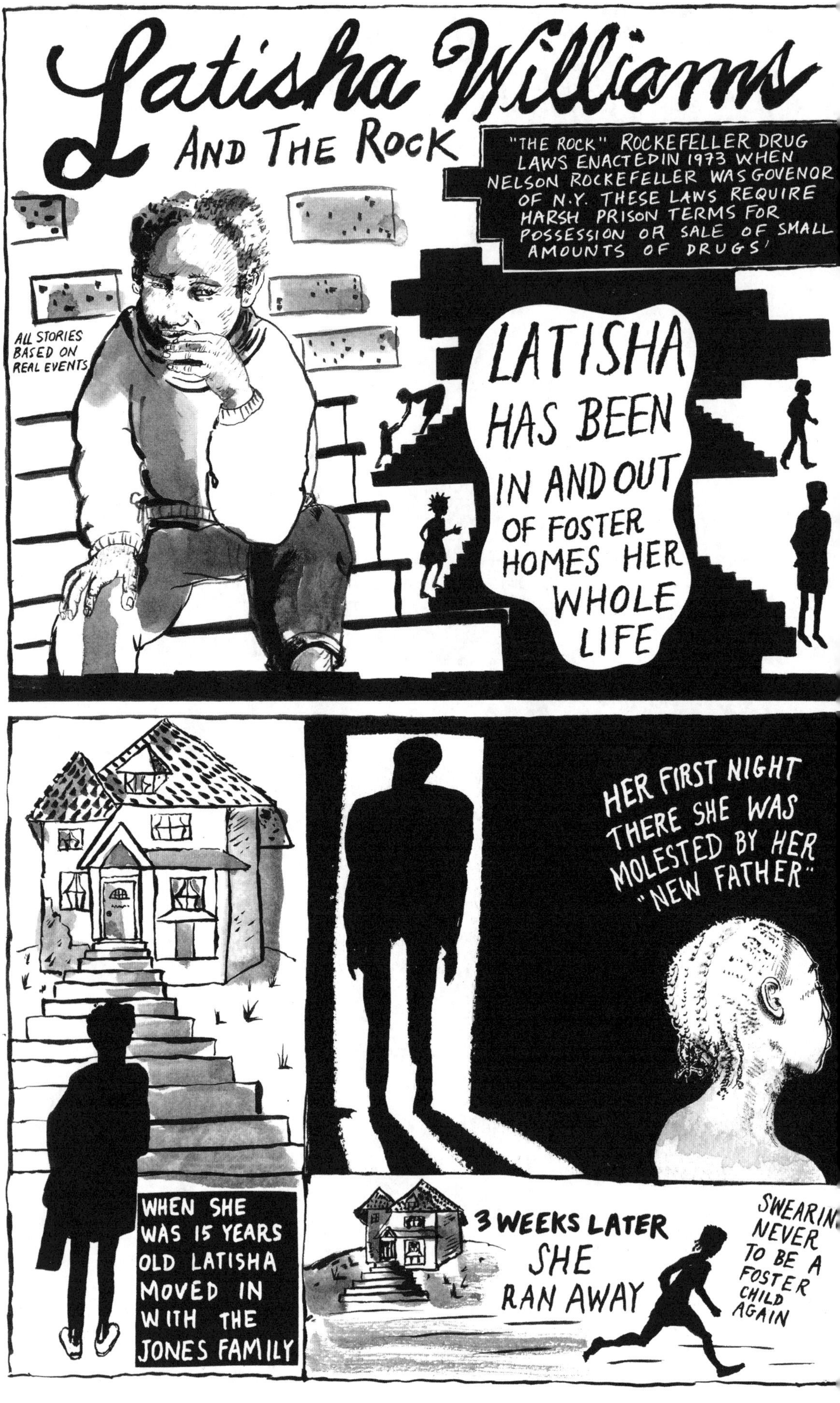

Latisha Williams
AND THE ROCK
"THE ROCK" ROCKEFELLER DRUG LAWS ENACTEDIN 1973 WHEN NELSON ROCKEFELLER WAS GOVENOR OF N.Y. THESE LAWS REQUIRE HARSH PRISON TERMS FOR POSSESSION OR SALE OF SMALL AMOUNTS OF DRUGS'
ALL STORIES BASED ON REAL EVENTS
LATISHA HAS BEEN IN AND OUT OF FOSTER HOMES HER WHOLE LIFE
WHEN SHE WAS 15 YEARS OLD LATISHA MOVED IN WITH THE JONES FAMILY
HER FIRST NIGHT THERE SHE WAS MOLESTED BY HER "NEW FATHER"
3 WEEKS LATER SHE RAN AWAY
SWEARIN NEVER TO BE A FOSTER CHILD AGAIN

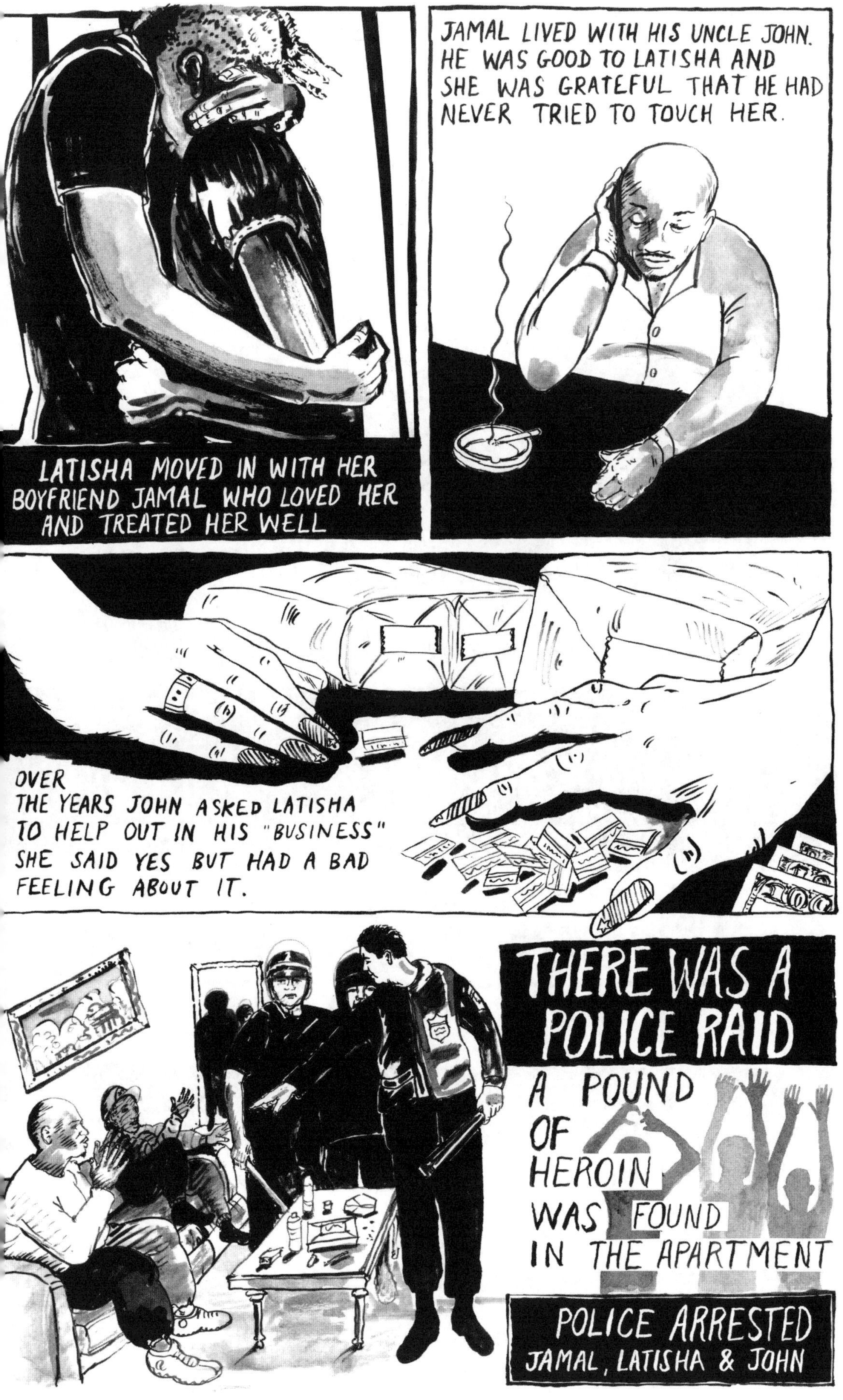
LATISHA MOVED IN WITH HER BOYFRIEND JAMAL WHO LOVED HER AND TREATED HER WELL
JAMAL LIVED WITH HIS UNCLE JOHN. HE WAS GOOD TO LATISHA AND SHE WAS GRATEFUL THAT HE HAD NEVER TRIED TO TOUCH HER.
OVER THE YEARS JOHN ASKED LATISHA TO HELP OUT IN HIS "BUSINESS" SHE SAID YES BUT HAD A BAD FEELING ABOUT IT.
THERE WAS A POLICE RAID
A POUND OF HEROIN WAS FOUND IN THE APARTMENT
POLICE ARRESTED JAMAL, LATISHA & JOHN

LATISHA WAS SENTENCED TO LIFE IN PRISON

WITH A MINIMUM OF 15 YEARS

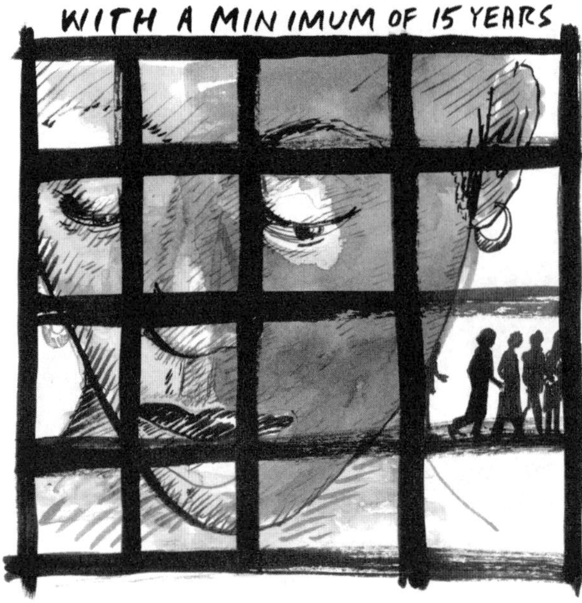

SHE WAS CHARGED WITH POSSESSION OF A POUND OF HEROIN A CLASS A-1 FELONY

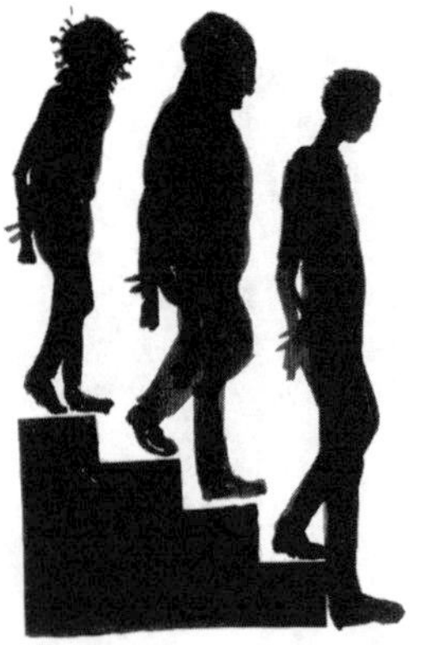

THE ROCK

THE MOST SERIOUS CLASSIFICATION OF A FELONY IN NEW YORK IS CLASS-A. THIS CATEGORY INCLUDE MURDER, KIDNAPPING, RAPE AND ARSON. IT ALSO INCLUDES THE POSSESSION OF 4 OUNCES OR SELLING OF 2 OUNCES OF A NARCOTIC DRUG (class A-1).

UNTIL THE "REFORM" OF THE ROCKEFELLER DRUG LAWS IN 12-04 THOSE CONVICTED OF CLASS A-1 FELONIES WERE GIVEN AN INDEFINITE PRISON TERM WITH 15 YEARS MINIMUM AND LIFE MAXIMUM NOW IT IS 8-20 YEARS. CURRENTLY ABOUT 450 PEOPLE LIKE LATISHA CAN APPEAL LEAVING 15,000 PEOPLE WITH DRUG FELONIES STILL INCARCERATED.

TAXPAYERS IN NEW YORK SPEND ABOUT $700,000,000 A YEAR TO KEEP PEOPLE CONVICTED OF DRUG CRIMES IN PRISON.

WHEN AND IF LATISHA GETS OUT OF PRISON

SHE WILL FACE HUGE OBSTACLES FINDING A JOB OR HOUSING BECAUSE OF HER CRIMINAL RECORD SHE WILL BE UNABLE TO GET A STUDENT LOAN OR LIVE IN PUBLIC HOUSING.

IN MANY STATES WOMEN WHO HAVE CRIMINAL RECORDS MAY NOT VOTE BECAUSE OF THIS

ONE IN EVERY 50 BLACK WOMEN IN AMERICA CANNOT VOTE[2]

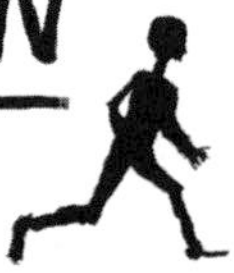

MORE THAN HALF OF THE WOMEN WHO GET OUT OF U.S. PRISONS **ARE NOT ALLOWED ACCESS TO PUBLIC BENEFITS**[3]

OVER 92,000 ARE SUBJECT TO A LIFE-TIME WELFARE BAN[4] INCLUDING FOOD STAMPS

IN NEW YORK STATE LATISHA COULD APPLY FOR WELFARE (TANF) BUT IN MANY OTHER STATES PEOPLE WITH DRUG RELATED FELONIES ARE DENIED WELFARE AND FOOD STAMPS PARTIALLY OR COMPLETELY.

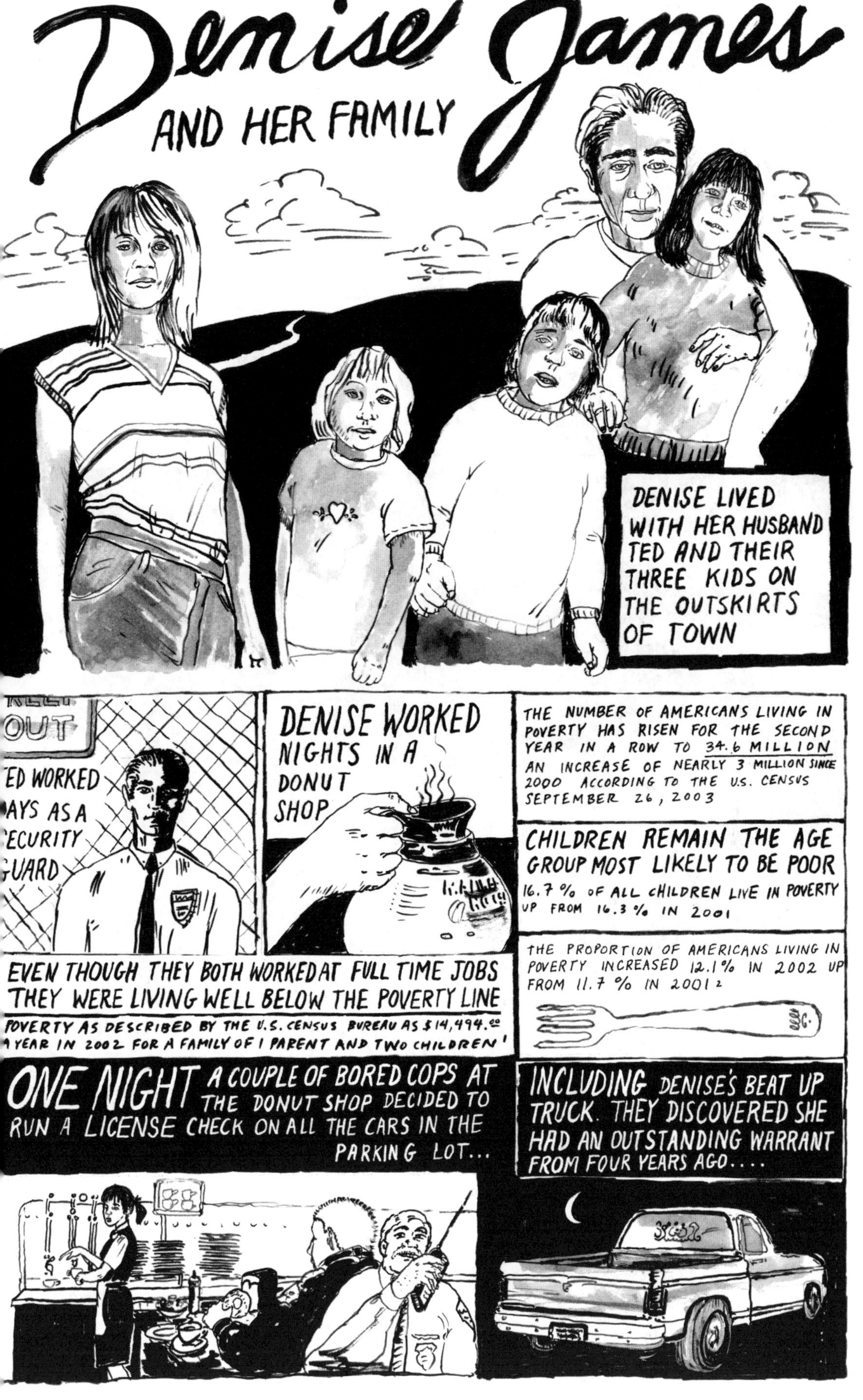

Denise James
AND HER FAMILY
DENISE LIVED WITH HER HUSBAND TED AND THEIR THREE KIDS ON THE OUTSKIRTS OF TOWN
OUT
ED WORKED
AYS AS A
ECURITY
UARD
DENISE WORKED NIGHTS IN A DONUT SHOP
THE NUMBER OF AMERICANS LIVING IN POVERTY HAS RISEN FOR THE SECOND YEAR IN A ROW TO 34.6 MILLION AN INCREASE OF NEARLY 3 MILLION SINCE 2000 ACCORDING TO THE U.S. CENSUS SEPTEMBER 26, 2003
CHILDREN REMAIN THE AGE GROUP MOST LIKELY TO BE POOR
16.7 % OF ALL CHILDREN LIVE IN POVERTY UP FROM 16.3 % IN 2001
EVEN THOUGH THEY BOTH WORKED AT FULL TIME JOBS THEY WERE LIVING WELL BELOW THE POVERTY LINE
POVERTY AS DESCRIBED BY THE U.S. CENSUS BUREAU AS $14,494.00 A YEAR IN 2002 FOR A FAMILY OF 1 PARENT AND TWO CHILDREN
THE PROPORTION OF AMERICANS LIVING IN POVERTY INCREASED 12.1% IN 2002 UP FROM 11.7 % IN 2001
ONE NIGHT A COUPLE OF BORED COPS AT THE DONUT SHOP DECIDED TO RUN A LICENSE CHECK ON ALL THE CARS IN THE PARKING LOT...
INCLUDING DENISE'S BEAT UP TRUCK. THEY DISCOVERED SHE HAD AN OUTSTANDING WARRANT FROM FOUR YEARS AGO....

DENISE WAS ARRESTED AND TAKEN TO JAIL

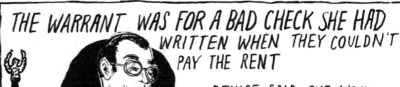

THE WARRANT WAS FOR A BAD CHECK SHE HAD WRITTEN WHEN THEY COULDN'T PAY THE RENT

DENISE SAID SHE WOULD PAY RESTITUTION... AS MUCH AS SHE COULD POSSIBLY AFFORD EACH MONTH

"SIX MONTHS IN JAIL..."

BUT THE JUDGE FELT HE HAD TO TEACH HER A LESSON.

INSTEAD OF ALLOWING DENISE TO PAY $900.00 IN RESTITUTION FOR BAD CHECKS IT WILL COST ABOUT $15,000.00 TO KEEP HER IN JAIL FOR 6 MONTHS

AFTER 6 MONTHS IN JAIL DENISE AND HER FAMILY WILL BE HOMELESS

TED COULDN'T PAY RENT WITH HIS INCOME ALONE

THE FAMILY WAS EVICTED FROM THEIR HOME

TED AND THE THREE KIDS MOVED INTO A MOTEL

OFFICE

VACANCY

THE CHILDREN HAD TO CHANGE SCHOOLS

TED: "... what am I gonna do? I can't keep up with the bills and the kids are doing so bad in school"

DENISE: "this is all my fault"

WHEN IT SEEMED THINGS COULDN'T GET WORSE A SCHOOL GUIDANCE COUNSELOR CALLED THE SOCIAL SERVICES

"... they appear to be homeless and uncared for..."

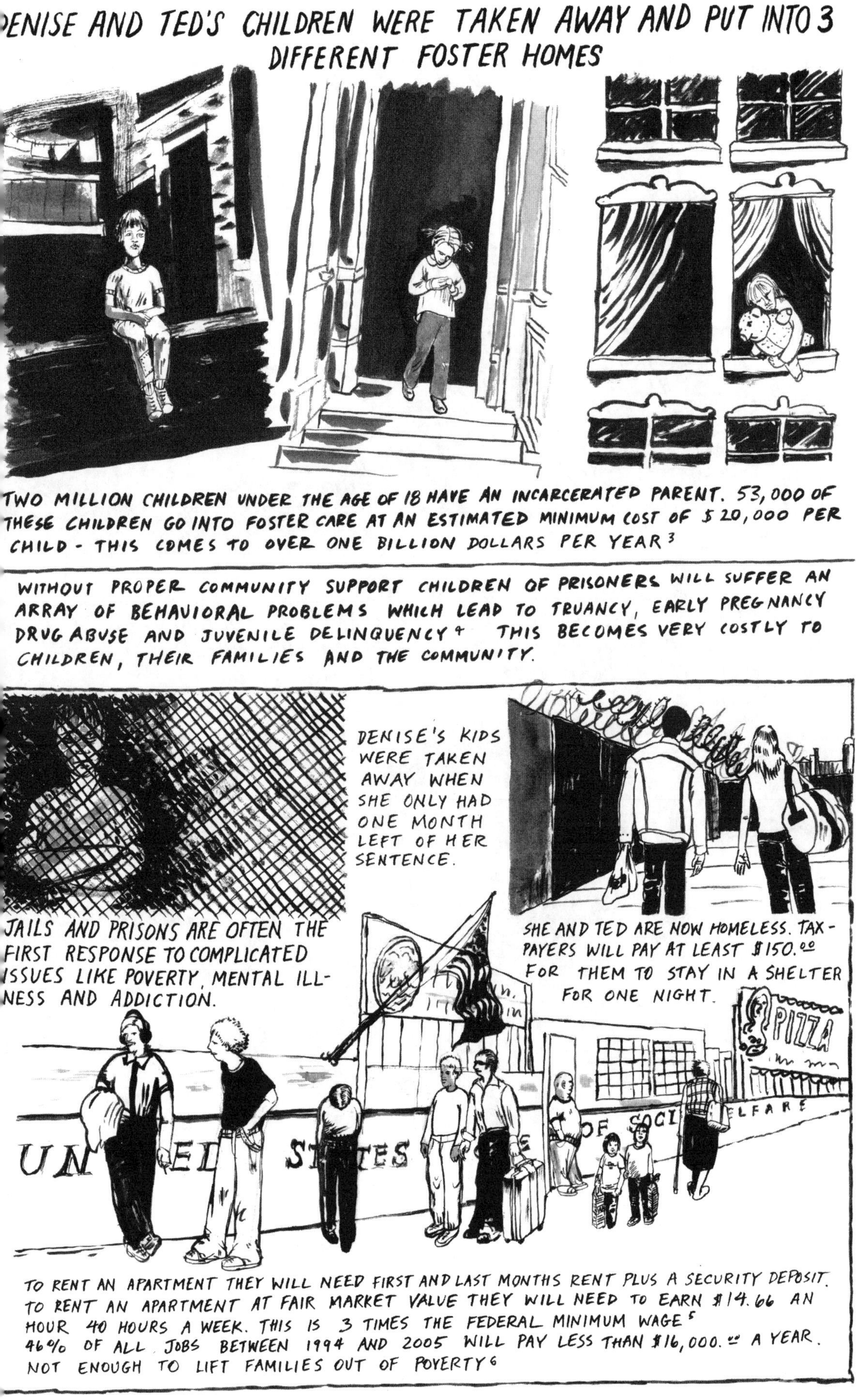
DENISE AND TED'S CHILDREN WERE TAKEN AWAY AND PUT INTO 3 DIFFERENT FOSTER HOMES
TWO MILLION CHILDREN UNDER THE AGE OF 18 HAVE AN INCARCERATED PARENT. 53,000 OF THESE CHILDREN GO INTO FOSTER CARE AT AN ESTIMATED MINIMUM COST OF $20,000 PER CHILD - THIS COMES TO OVER ONE BILLION DOLLARS PER YEAR[3]
WITHOUT PROPER COMMUNITY SUPPORT CHILDREN OF PRISONERS WILL SUFFER AN ARRAY OF BEHAVIORAL PROBLEMS WHICH LEAD TO TRUANCY, EARLY PREGNANCY DRUG ABUSE AND JUVENILE DELINQUENCY[4] THIS BECOMES VERY COSTLY TO CHILDREN, THEIR FAMILIES AND THE COMMUNITY.
DENISE'S KIDS WERE TAKEN AWAY WHEN SHE ONLY HAD ONE MONTH LEFT OF HER SENTENCE.
JAILS AND PRISONS ARE OFTEN THE FIRST RESPONSE TO COMPLICATED ISSUES LIKE POVERTY, MENTAL ILLNESS AND ADDICTION.
SHE AND TED ARE NOW HOMELESS. TAXPAYERS WILL PAY AT LEAST $150.00 FOR THEM TO STAY IN A SHELTER FOR ONE NIGHT.
PIZZA
TO RENT AN APARTMENT THEY WILL NEED FIRST AND LAST MONTHS RENT PLUS A SECURITY DEPOSIT. TO RENT AN APARTMENT AT FAIR MARKET VALUE THEY WILL NEED TO EARN $14.66 AN HOUR 40 HOURS A WEEK. THIS IS 3 TIMES THE FEDERAL MINIMUM WAGE[5]
46% OF ALL JOBS BETWEEN 1994 AND 2005 WILL PAY LESS THAN $16,000.00 A YEAR. NOT ENOUGH TO LIFT FAMILIES OUT OF POVERTY[6]

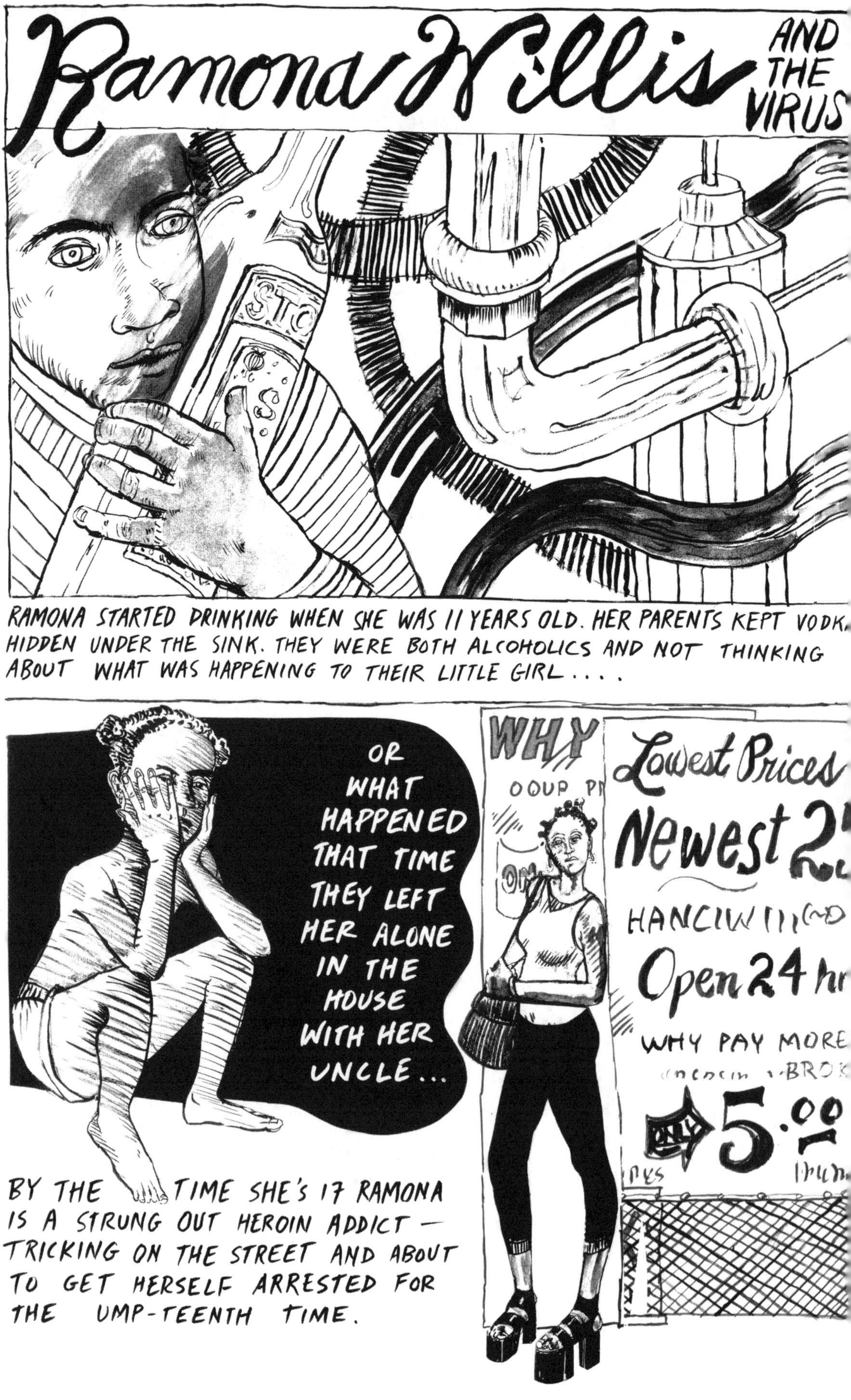
Ramona Willis AND THE VIRUS
STO
RAMONA STARTED DRINKING WHEN SHE WAS 11 YEARS OLD. HER PARENTS KEPT VODKA HIDDEN UNDER THE SINK. THEY WERE BOTH ALCOHOLICS AND NOT THINKING ABOUT WHAT WAS HAPPENING TO THEIR LITTLE GIRL....
OR WHAT HAPPENED THAT TIME THEY LEFT HER ALONE IN THE HOUSE WITH HER UNCLE...
WHY
Lowest Prices
Newest
Open 24
WHY PAY MORE
ONLY
5.00
BY THE TIME SHE'S 17 RAMONA IS A STRUNG OUT HEROIN ADDICT — TRICKING ON THE STREET AND ABOUT TO GET HERSELF ARRESTED FOR THE UMP-TEENTH TIME.

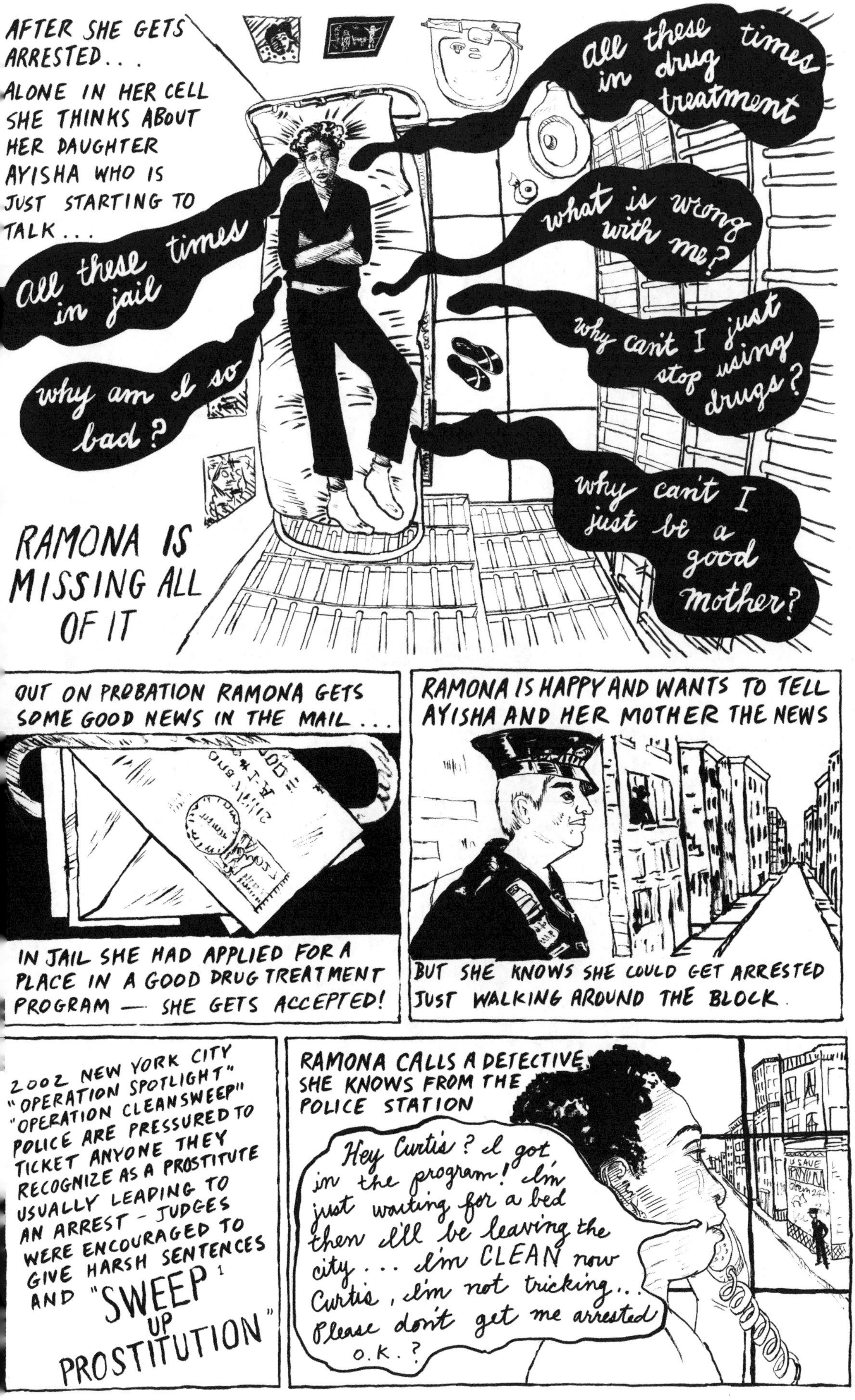
AFTER SHE GETS ARRESTED...
ALONE IN HER CELL SHE THINKS ABOUT HER DAUGHTER AYISHA WHO IS JUST STARTING TO TALK...
All these times in jail
why am I so bad?
All these times in drug treatment
what is wrong with me?
why can't I just stop using drugs?
why can't I just be a good mother?
RAMONA IS MISSING ALL OF IT
OUT ON PROBATION RAMONA GETS SOME GOOD NEWS IN THE MAIL...
IN JAIL SHE HAD APPLIED FOR A PLACE IN A GOOD DRUG TREATMENT PROGRAM — SHE GETS ACCEPTED!
RAMONA IS HAPPY AND WANTS TO TELL AYISHA AND HER MOTHER THE NEWS
BUT SHE KNOWS SHE COULD GET ARRESTED JUST WALKING AROUND THE BLOCK.
2002 NEW YORK CITY "OPERATION SPOTLIGHT" "OPERATION CLEANSWEEP" POLICE ARE PRESSURED TO TICKET ANYONE THEY RECOGNIZE AS A PROSTITUTE USUALLY LEADING TO AN ARREST - JUDGES WERE ENCOURAGED TO GIVE HARSH SENTENCES AND "SWEEP UP PROSTITUTION"[1]
RAMONA CALLS A DETECTIVE SHE KNOWS FROM THE POLICE STATION
Hey Curtis? I got in the program! I'm just waiting for a bed then I'll be leaving the city... I'm CLEAN now Curtis, I'm not tricking... Please don't get me arrested O.K.?

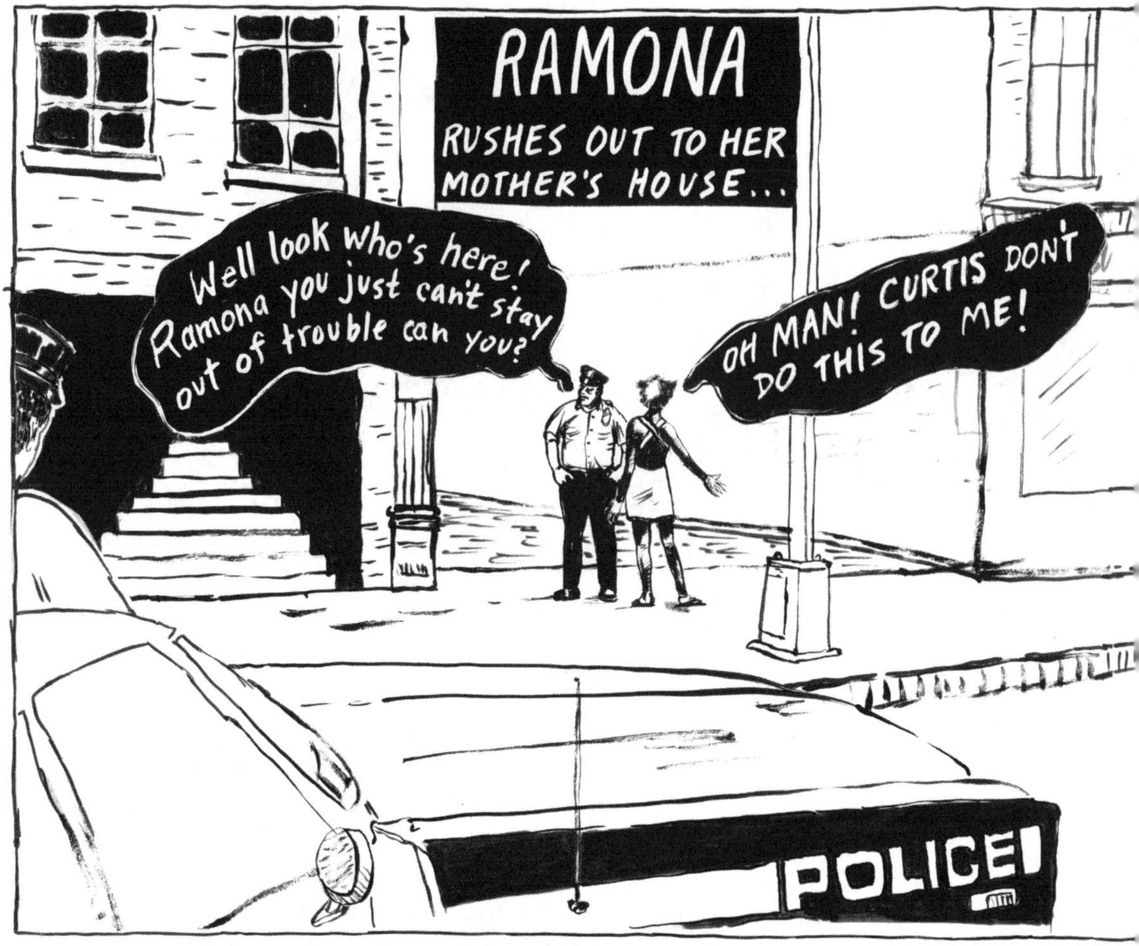
RAMONA
RUSHES OUT TO HER MOTHER'S HOUSE...
Well look who's here! Ramona you just can't stay out of trouble can you?
OH MAN! CURTIS DON'T DO THIS TO ME!
POLICE

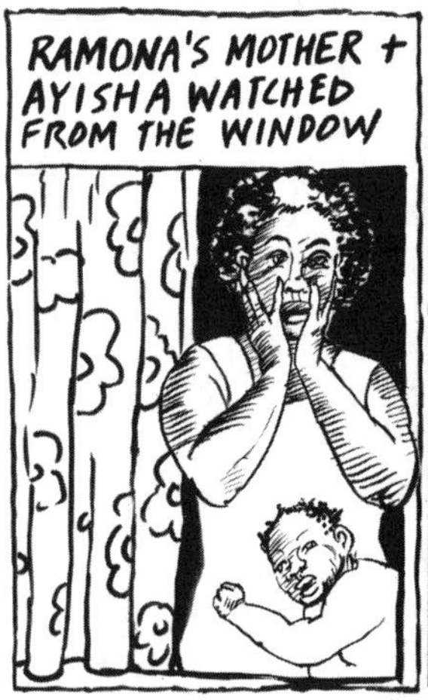
RAMONA'S MOTHER + AYISHA WATCHED FROM THE WINDOW

ONE IN FIVE

CHILDREN OF WOMEN WHO BECOME INCARCERATED WILL WITNESS THEIR MOTHER'S ARREST. FEW POLICIES ARE IN PLACE TO MAKE SURE THESE CHILDREN'S NEEDS ARE MET[2]

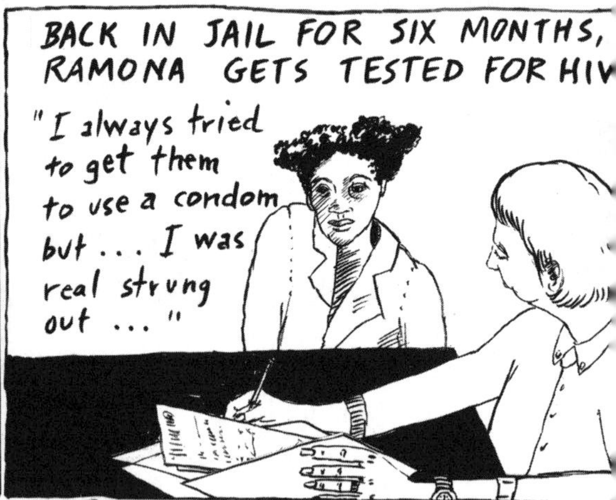
BACK IN JAIL FOR SIX MONTHS, RAMONA GETS TESTED FOR HIV
"I always tried to get them to use a condom but . . . I was real strung out . . ."

WHILE SHE WAITS FOR HER RESULTS TO COME BACK, RAMONA PARTICIPATES AS MUCH AS SHE CAN IN THE UNIT ACTIVITIES.

SHE GOES TO G.E.D. CLASSES.

SHE STARTS WORK AT A PAID JOB.

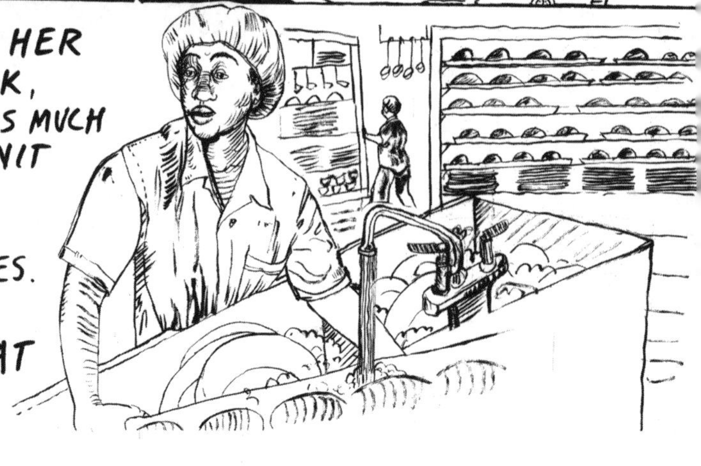

RAMONA'S TEST RESULTS ARE POSITIVE

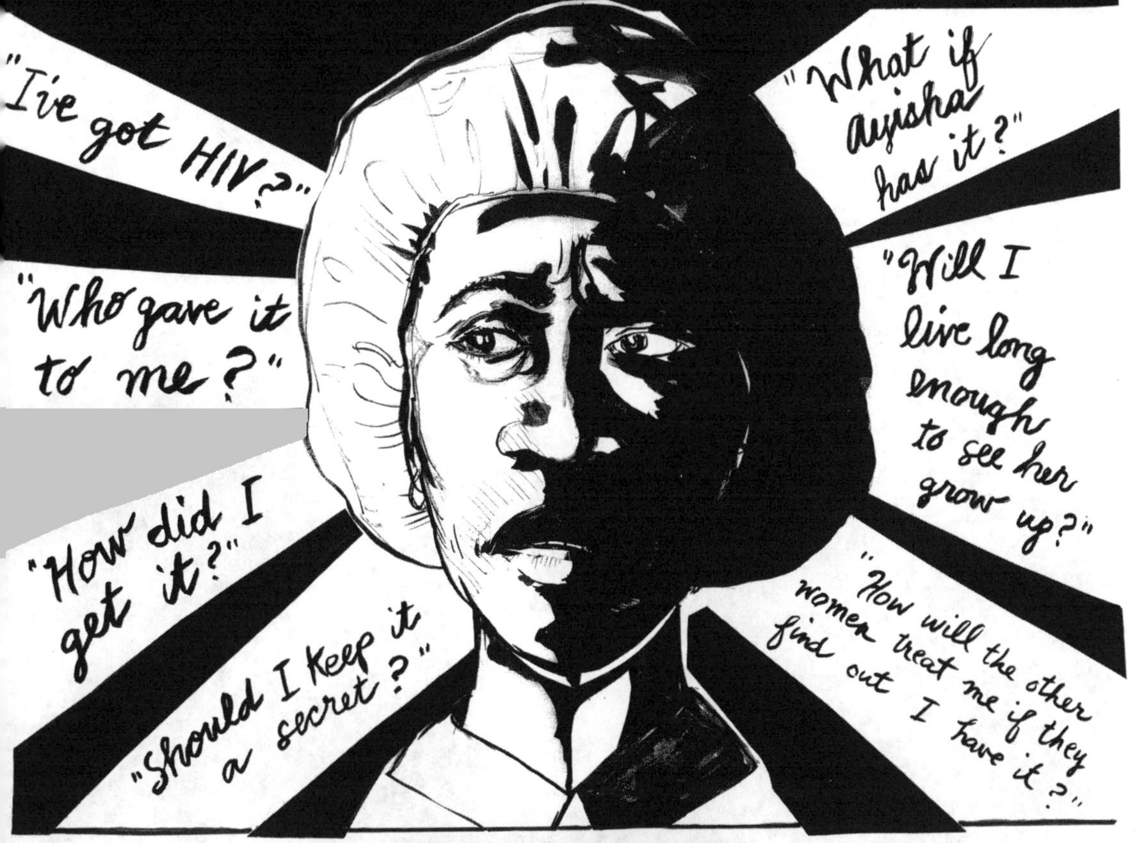
"I've got HIV?"
"Who gave it to me?"
"How did I get it?"
"Should I keep it a secret?"
"What if Ayisha has it?"
"Will I live long enough to see her grow up?"
"How will the other women treat me if they find out I have it?"

3.6%
OF ALL WOMEN INCARCERATED IN THE U.S. ARE HIV+
THAT IS 12 TIMES THE NATIONAL RATE.

WOMEN IN PRISON HAVE A VERY HIGH RATE OF HIV.

18%
OF ALL WOMEN INCARCERATED IN NY STATE ARE HIV+
THAT IS <u>60</u> TIMES THE NATIONAL RATE.[3]

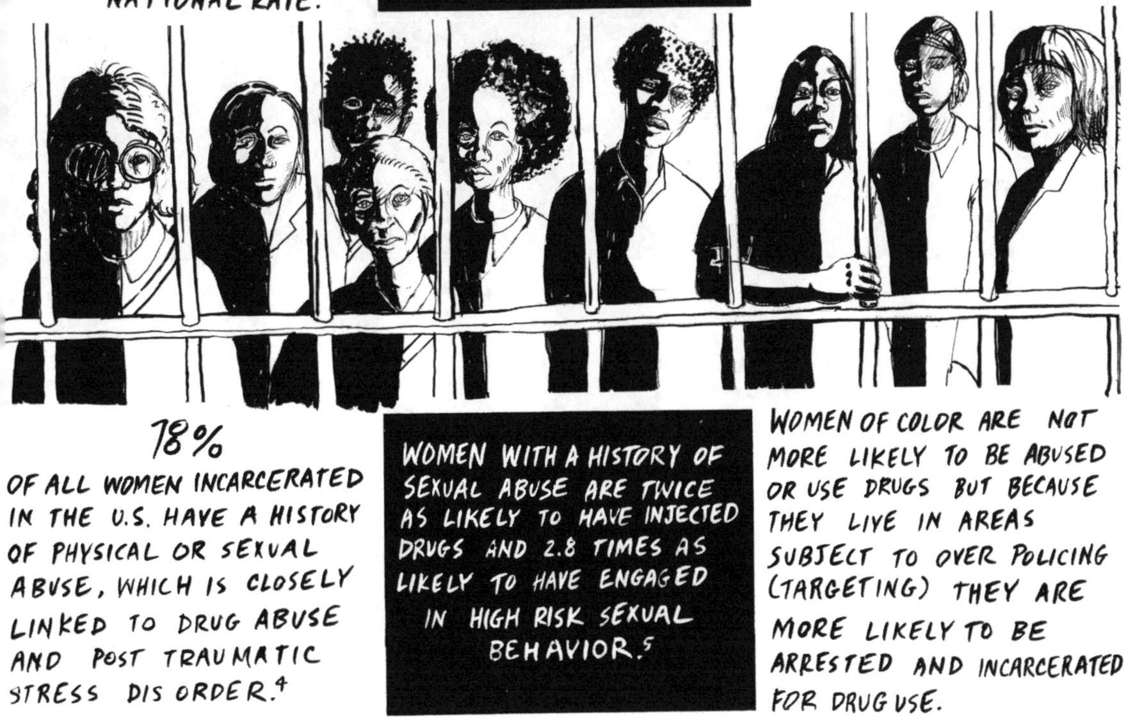

78%
OF ALL WOMEN INCARCERATED IN THE U.S. HAVE A HISTORY OF PHYSICAL OR SEXUAL ABUSE, WHICH IS CLOSELY LINKED TO DRUG ABUSE AND POST TRAUMATIC STRESS DISORDER.[4]

WOMEN WITH A HISTORY OF SEXUAL ABUSE ARE TWICE AS LIKELY TO HAVE INJECTED DRUGS AND 2.8 TIMES AS LIKELY TO HAVE ENGAGED IN HIGH RISK SEXUAL BEHAVIOR.[5]

WOMEN OF COLOR ARE NOT MORE LIKELY TO BE ABUSED OR USE DRUGS BUT BECAUSE THEY LIVE IN AREAS SUBJECT TO OVER POLICING (TARGETING) THEY ARE MORE LIKELY TO BE ARRESTED AND INCARCERATED FOR DRUG USE.

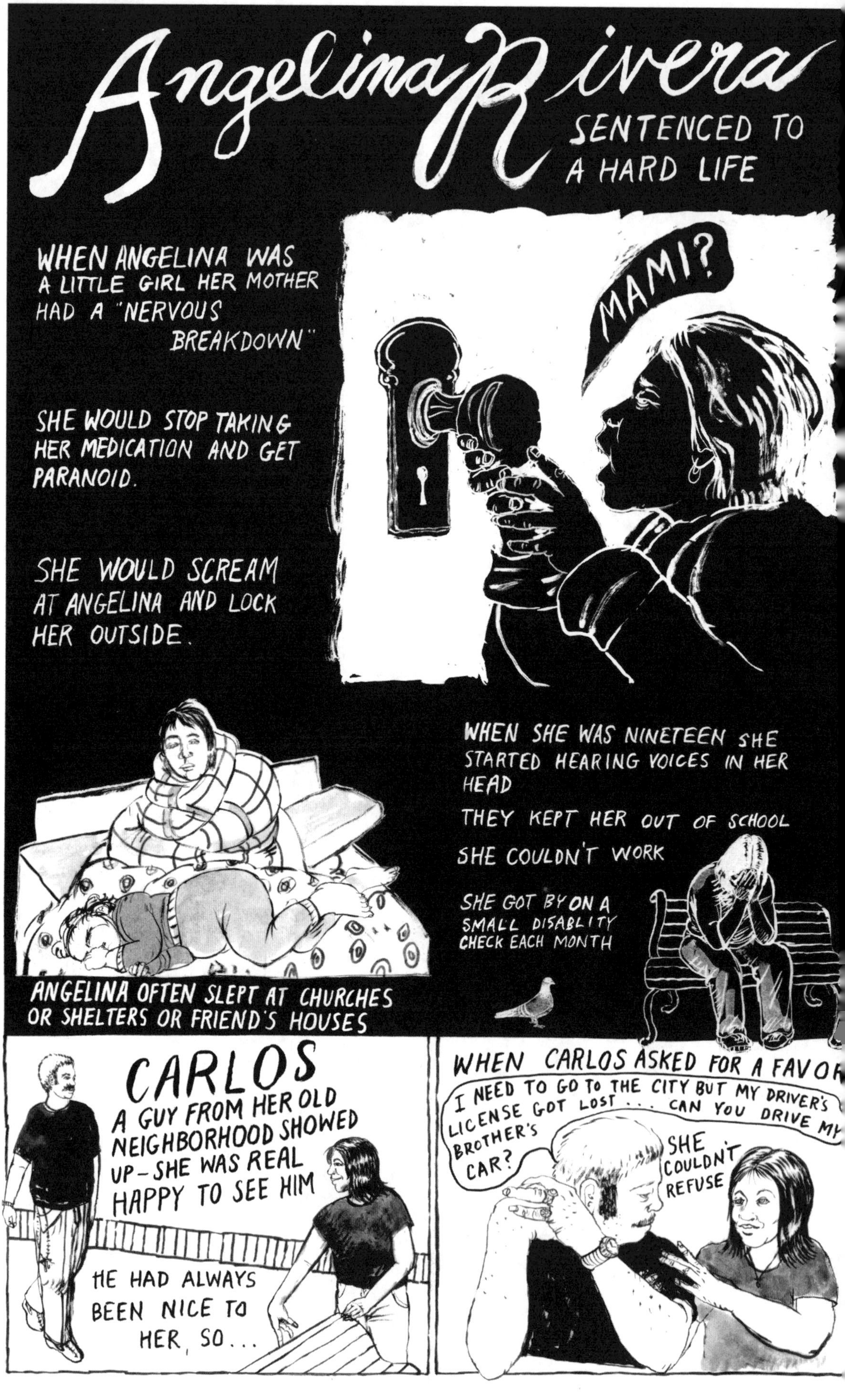
Angelina Rivera
SENTENCED TO A HARD LIFE
WHEN ANGELINA WAS A LITTLE GIRL HER MOTHER HAD A "NERVOUS BREAKDOWN"
SHE WOULD STOP TAKING HER MEDICATION AND GET PARANOID.
SHE WOULD SCREAM AT ANGELINA AND LOCK HER OUTSIDE.
MAMI?
ANGELINA OFTEN SLEPT AT CHURCHES OR SHELTERS OR FRIEND'S HOUSES
WHEN SHE WAS NINETEEN SHE STARTED HEARING VOICES IN HER HEAD
THEY KEPT HER OUT OF SCHOOL
SHE COULDN'T WORK
SHE GOT BY ON A SMALL DISABLITY CHECK EACH MONTH
CARLOS
A GUY FROM HER OLD NEIGHBORHOOD SHOWED UP-SHE WAS REAL HAPPY TO SEE HIM
HE HAD ALWAYS BEEN NICE TO HER, SO...
WHEN CARLOS ASKED FOR A FAVOR
I NEED TO GO TO THE CITY BUT MY DRIVER'S LICENSE GOT LOST . . . CAN YOU DRIVE MY BROTHER'S CAR?
SHE COULDN'T REFUSE

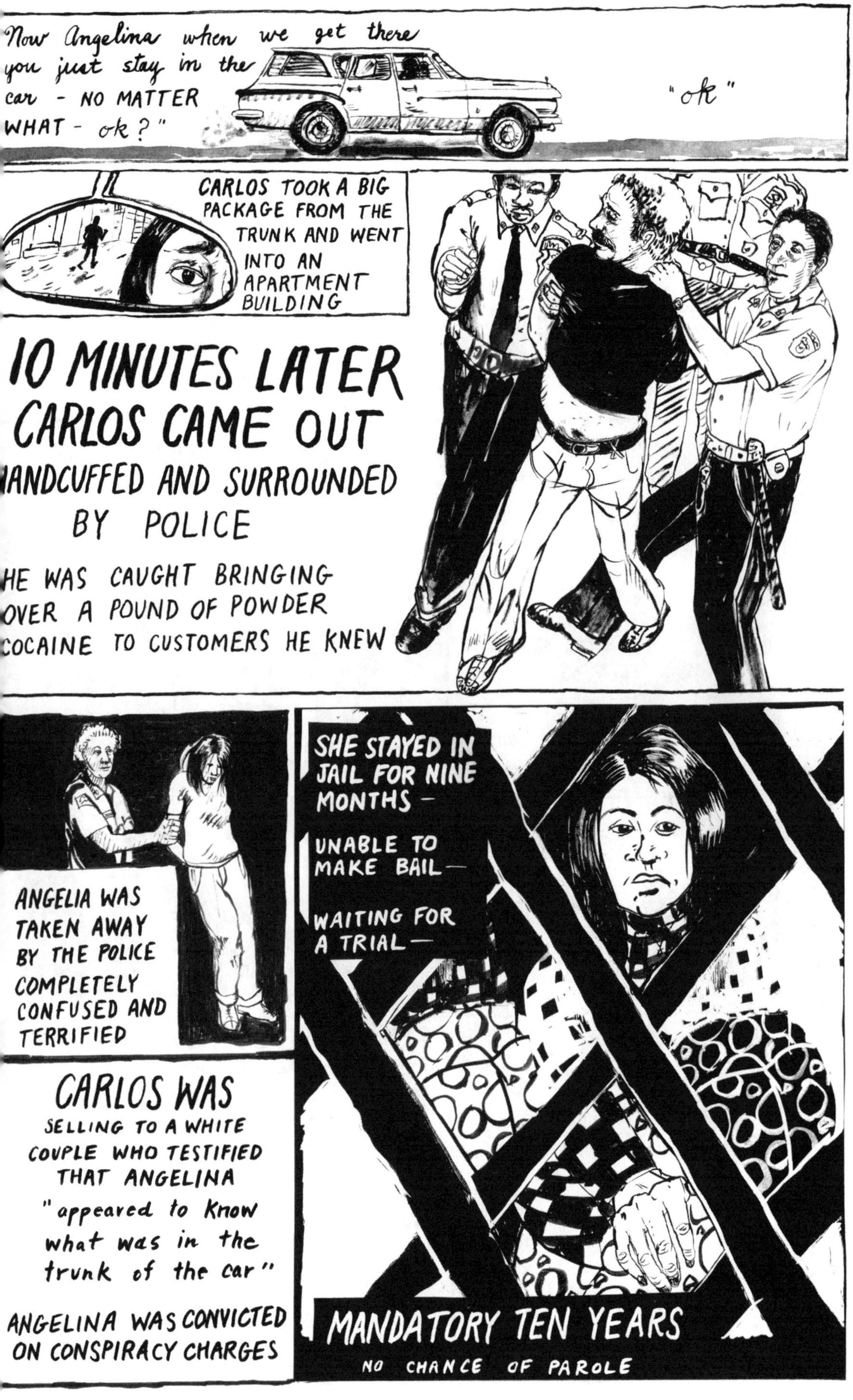

Now Angelina when we get there you just stay in the car - NO MATTER WHAT - ok?"
"ok"
CARLOS TOOK A BIG PACKAGE FROM THE TRUNK AND WENT INTO AN APARTMENT BUILDING
10 MINUTES LATER CARLOS CAME OUT HANDCUFFED AND SURROUNDED BY POLICE
HE WAS CAUGHT BRINGING OVER A POUND OF POWDER COCAINE TO CUSTOMERS HE KNEW
ANGELIA WAS TAKEN AWAY BY THE POLICE COMPLETELY CONFUSED AND TERRIFIED
SHE STAYED IN JAIL FOR NINE MONTHS —
UNABLE TO MAKE BAIL —
WAITING FOR A TRIAL —
CARLOS WAS SELLING TO A WHITE COUPLE WHO TESTIFIED THAT ANGELINA "appeared to know what was in the trunk of the car"
ANGELINA WAS CONVICTED ON CONSPIRACY CHARGES
MANDATORY TEN YEARS
NO CHANCE OF PAROLE

WOMEN SENTENCED WITH DRUG CONSRIRACY HAVE OFTEN BEEN USED AS COURIERS OR "DRUG MULES"

SINCE THEY DON'T HAVE INFORMATION ABOUT THE DEALERS TO TRADE OR "PLEA BARGAIN" THEY END UP WITH LONGER SENTENCES.

EVEN WHEN THEY ARE INNOCENT WOMEN WITHOUT MONEY HAVE TROUBLE FINDING GOOD LEGAL DEFENSE.

CARLOS GOT A SHORTER SENTENCE THAN ANGELINA. HE TRADED INFO ABOUT OTHER DEALERS AND CUSTOMERS FOR A REDUCED SENTENCE.

IN THIS CASE THE DRUG BUYERS DIDN'T GO TO JAIL AT ALL. THEY WERE FEDERAL UNDERCOVER AGENTS.

WOMEN WHO HAVE BEEN ABUSED OR NEGLECTED AS CHILDREN HAVE A 77% HIGHER RATE OF ARREST THAN WOMEN WHO WERE NOT ABUSED

78% OF ALL INCARCERATED WOMEN WERE ABUSED AS A CHILD.

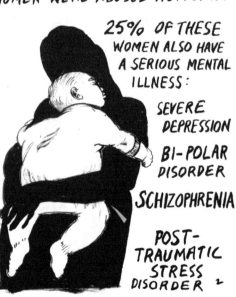

25% OF THESE WOMEN ALSO HAVE A SERIOUS MENTAL ILLNESS:

SEVERE DEPRESSION

BI-POLAR DISORDER

SCHIZOPHRENIA

POST-TRAUMATIC STRESS DISORDER [2]

THE COST OF KEEPING ONE PERSON IN PRISON FOR ONE YEAR IS $29,000

$290,000 OF OUR TAXES WILL BE SPENT TO KEEP ANGELINA LOCKED UP

FOR EVERY 1000 WOMEN IN AMERICA:

36 IMPRISONED WOMEN ARE BLACK
15 IMPRISONED WOMEN ARE HISPANIC
5 IMPRISONED WOMEN ARE WHITE [3]

REGINA MCKNIGHT

REGINA McKNIGHT IS IN PRISON IN SOUTH CAROLINA BECAUSE THE STATE ATTORNEY GENERAL THINKS SHE HAS COMMITTED **MURDER**.

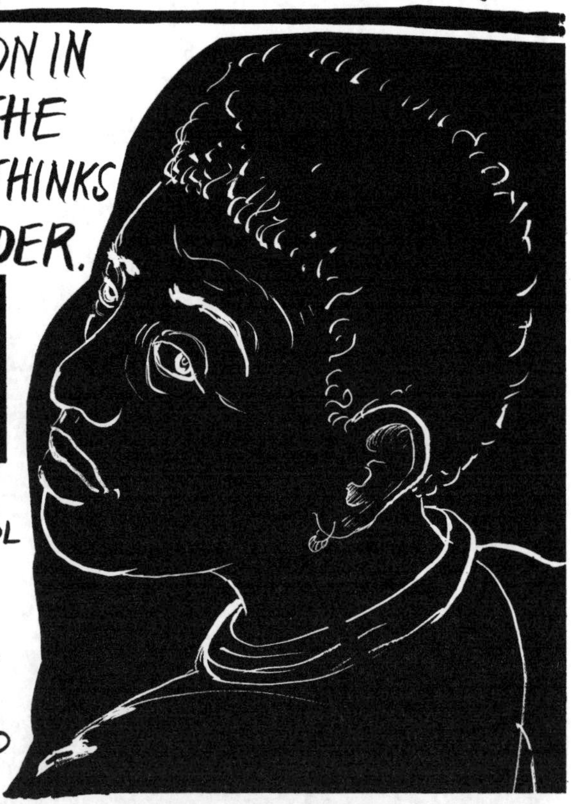

SHE IS THE FIRST WOMAN IN AMERICA TO BE CONVICTED OF MURDER BECAUSE OF HER BEHAVIOR WHILE PREGNANT.

REGINA IS A 27 YEAR OLD AFRICAN-AMERICAN WOMAN WHO LEFT SCHOOL AFTER 10th GRADE AND WENT TO WORK ON A TOBACCO FARM. WHEN HER MOTHER WAS KILLED BY A HIT AND RUN DRIVER SHE BECAME HOMELESS AND ADDICTED TO DRUGS.

IN 1999 SHE WAS PREGNANT WITH HER THIRD CHILD, A GIRL SHE'D NAMED MERCEDES. THE BABY WAS DELIVERED STILLBORN. WHEN AN AUTOPSY FOUND TRACES OF COCAINE IN THE FETUS, REGINA WAS ARRESTED AND PUT ON TRIAL FOR MURDER.

EVEN THOUGH THERE IS NO MEDICAL EVIDENCE THAT COCAINE USE CAUSES STILLBIRTH AND A LARGE PERCENTAGE OF STILLBIRTHS HAVE ***NO OBVIOUS CAUSE***, REGINA WAS TRIED FOR THE DEATH OF HER OWN FETUS.

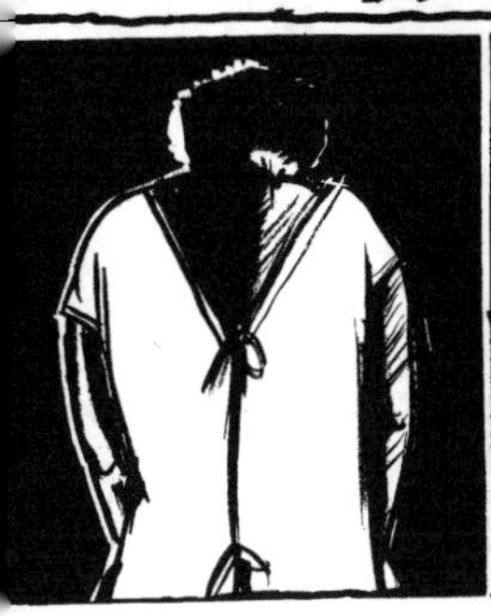

SHE WAS TRIED UNDER SOUTH CAROLINA'S "HOMICIDE BY CHILD ABUSE" LAW WHICH CAN BE APPLIED TO A FETUS. IN SOUTH CAROLINA A "VIABLE FETUS" IS A PERSON FOR PURPOSES OF PROSECUTION.

DURING REGINA'S TRIAL THE STATE'S OWN EXPERTS TESTIFIED THAT THEY COULDN'T SAY FOR CERTAIN IF COCAINE USE HAD CAUSED REGINA'S STILLBIRTH. MANY TESTS THAT SHOULD HAVE BEEN DONE WERE NOT DONE. WHEN TWO JURORS ADMITTED TO USING THE INTERNET TO RESEARCH THE CASE A MISTRIAL WAS DECLARED.

AT THE RETRIAL THE SAME EXPERTS WITH NO NEW EVIDENCE CLAIMED THAT COCAINE WAS THE DEFINITE CAUSE FOR REGINA'S STILLBIRTH.

THE JURY CONSIDERED THE CASE FOR 15 MINUTES

REGINA WAS FOUND GUILTY OF HOMICIDE BY CHILD ABUSE AND SENTENCED TO 20 YEARS WITH 8 SUSPENDED.

THE CASE WAS APPEALED TO THE STATE SUPREME COURT MANY MEDICAL AND PUBLIC HEALTH GROUPS TRIED TO SUPPORT REGINA'S CASE FILING NUMEROUS STATEMENTS EXPLAINING HOW COCAINE USE ALONE COULD NOT CAUSE THE STILLBIRTH.

PROSECUTORS ADMITTED THAT REGINA HAD NO INTENTION OF HARMING HER PREGNANCY, AND YET THEY UPHELD HER SENTENCE OF MURDER. THIS WAS ESSENTIALLY BECAUSE SHE WAS A DRUG USER WHICH THE COURT INTERPRETED AS SHOWING:

EXTREME INDIFFERENCE TO HUMAN LIFE...

THEY ALSO STATED THAT REGINA WOULD BENEFIT FROM DRUG ABUSE TREATMENT BUT WITH LIMITED RESOURCES AVAILABLE IN SOUTH CAROLINA FOR DRUG ABUSE PROGRAMS SHE WENT TO PRISON INSTEAD.

— FALL 2003 U.S. SUPREME COURT DECIDES NOT TO HEAR THE CASE. IT IS STILL ON APPEAL

— SINCE 1985 OVER 200 WOMEN HAVE BEEN ARRESTED ON THE GROUNDS THAT THEIR BEHAVIOR JEOPARDIZED THEIR PREGNANCY. 1

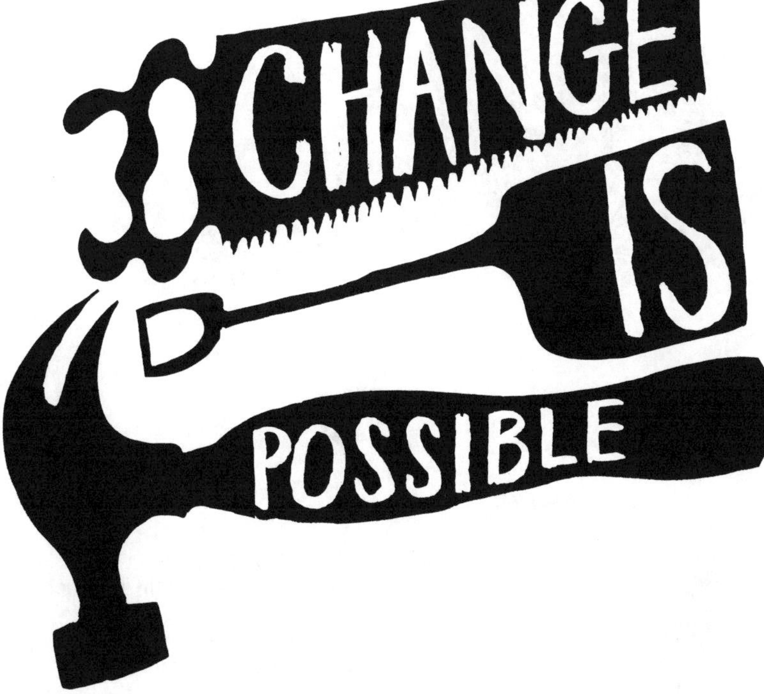
CHANGE
IS
POSSIBLE

PRISONS AND JAILS

Stop building new prisons and jails and close others down. Re-direct the $57 billion[1] spent on jails and prisons to quality education, housing, job training, daycare and health care.

ALTERNATIVES TO JAIL[2]

Citation Programs—Give tickets to those committing misdemeanor or low-level crimes without booking them through the arrest process.

Improve Release Procedures for the Pretrial and Sentenced Populations—These improvements decrease jail populations by ensuring that people are moving through the system in a timely fashion.

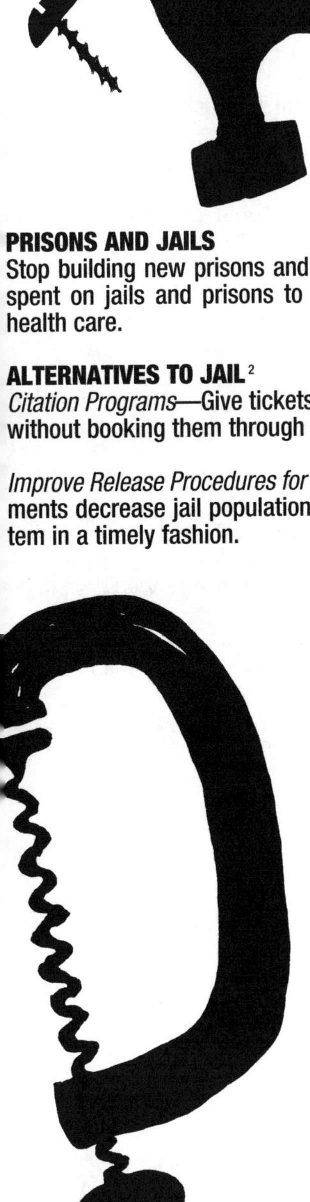

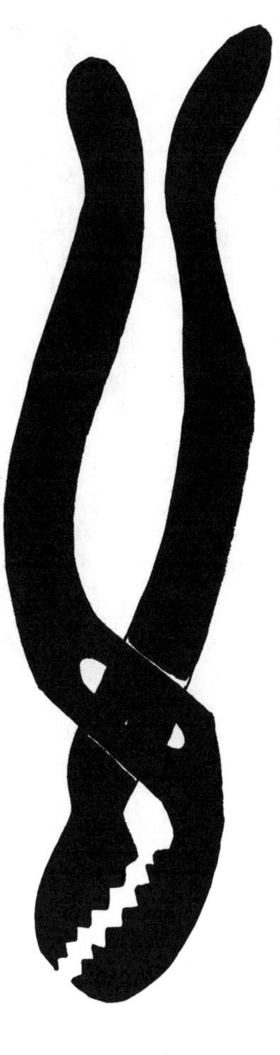

Pre-Trial Diversion—Pretrial services programs can help alleviate jail crowding by releasing people who are incarcerated before trial.

Bail Reform—National studies show most people being held pretrial cannot post a money bond or bail.

Specialty Courts—Drug courts, domestic violence courts and mental health courts and other specialty courts were developed to provide individuals involved with the criminal justice system with treatment.

Alternatives to Incarceration in Jail—In response to increased jail populations, probation agencies need to work with other criminal justice agencies to develop alternative programs.

Probation and Parole—Missed appointments with a parole officer, breaking curfew or a failed drug test should not be the reason to send someone back to prison. Instead, treatment should be offered through diversion programs.

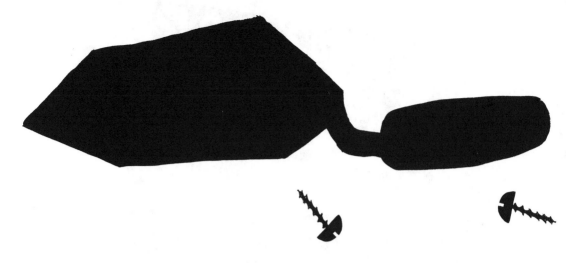

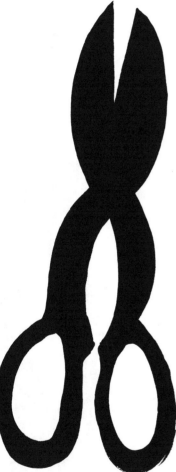

FAMILIES [3]

States should:

Actively encourage kinship care placements

Ensure that child welfare authorities remain in touch with incarcerated parents.

Facilitate visitation between children and incarcerated parents.

Make reunification services available to parents.

Explore alternatives to incarceration that could make child welfare intervention and child removal unnecessary in many cases.

Ensure that incarcerated parents have the opportunity to attend all hearings in their cases.

Provide incarcerated parents with legal services.

DRUG POLICY [4]

Repeal mandatory sentencing laws. See the Glossary for a definition and learn more about the injustices of mandatory sentences by contacting Families against Mandatory Minimums.

WOMEN BACK HOME [5]

Modify restrictive public housing and Section 8 guidelines to allow formerly incarcerated women access to affordable housing.

Lift the ban on welfare (TANF and food stamps) for people with drug felony convictions.

Repeal the ban on student financial aid which was passed as part of the 1998 reauthorization of Higher Education Act of 1965. It keeps anyone convicted of a drug felony from getting college loans.

Make work more possible for people coming out of jails and prisons. Examples include: expunging offenses, sealing records, offering certificates of rehabilitation. Eliminate discrimination by prospective employers.

DISENFRANCHISEMENT

All citizens should have the right to vote including those who are incarcerated, on probation and on parole.

WORK TO DESTIGMATIZE AND DECRIMINALIZE "SEX WORK."

DRUG AND ALCOHOL TREATMENT

Shift funding priorities from the $167 billion for law enforcement, courts, prisons and jails to comprehensive women-focused drug and alcohol treatment. From 1997 to 2001 state and local spending for corrections rose 1101%. Spending for education rose 470%. Spending for healthcare and hospitals rose 482%. [6]

NEEDLE EXCHANGE

Encourage and fund needle exchange programs to help stop the spread of Hepatitis C and HIV.

PREVENTING AND TREATMENT FOR SEXUAL AND PHYSICAL ABUSE [7]

Untreated physical and sexual abuse contributes to mental illness and drug abuse. According to the WPA 12/03 report, "Women with a history of sexual abuse are twice as likely as non-abused women to have injected drugs." Early identification, treatment and prevention of sexual and physical abuse would significantly make the lives of girls and women more productive and positive.

INVEST IN QUALITY EDUCATION, JOB TRAINING FOR WORK THAT PAYS A LIVING WAGE, AFFORDABLE SAFE HOUSING, RELIABLE PUBLICLY FUNDED DAY CARE FOR EVERYONE WHO NEEDS IT.

JUSTICE REINVESTMENT/COMMUNITY REINVESTMENT [8]

Justice reinvestment is the creation of safer and viable communities by communities taking control of justice dollars and reallocating them to finance education, housing, healthcare and jobs.

1. Bureau of Justice Statistics Bulletin, Justice Expenditure and Employment in the U.S., May 2004; 2. Thanks to Dana Kaplan, National Resource Center on Prisons and Communities, Cincinnati, OH 2/04; 3. Barriers Facing Parents with Criminal Records/ Center for Law and Policy CLASP, 2003. www.clasp.org; 4. Families Against Mandatory Minimums, www.famm.org; 5. Women's Prison Association: Dina Rose, WPA Focus on Women and Justice October 2003, wpaonline.org; 6. Bureau of Justice Statistics Bulletin, Justice Expenditure and Employment in the U.S., May 2004; 7. WPA Focus on Women and Justice 12/03; 8. "Justice Reinvestment" by Susan B. Tucker and Eric Cadora, Ideas for an Open Society, 11/03. www.soros.org.

FOR MORE DETAILED INFORMATION ABOUT THE ORGANIZATIONS WORKING ON EACH OF THESE AND OTHER ISSUES, VISIT THE REAL COST OF PRISONS WEBSITE AT WWW.REALCOSTOFPRISONS.ORG.

PAGE ONE
1. Sokoloff, "Violent Female Offenders in NY State: Myths and Facts," *Crime and Justice in NY,* A. Karmon, 2001-02.
2. *Project on Incarcerated Mothers and Their Children,* Vol. 1, #1, 8/03. Harris School for Public Policy.
3. "Incarcerated Parents and Their Children," Christopher Mumola, *Bureau of Justice Statistics Special Report,* 8/00.
4. *Incarcerated Mothers and Their Children,* Vol. 1, #1, 8/03.
5. Ibid.
6. *Report of the Reentry Policy Council: Charting the Safe and Successful Release of Prisoners to the Community,* 1/05.
7. *Human Rights Watch,* 5/00.
8. MALDEF, 12/03.
9. WPA, "Focus on Women and Justice—A Portrait of Women in Prison," 12/03.
10. Drop the Rock, www.droptherock.org.

LATISHA WILLIAMS AND THE ROCK
1. Drop the Rock, www.droptherock.org.
2. The Sentencing Project, "Felony Disenfranchisement Rates for Women," 8/04.
3. WPA, "Focus on Women and Justice— Barriers to Re-entry," 10/03.
4. The Sentencing Project, "Life Sentences: Denying Welfare Benefits to Women Convicted of Drug Offences," 1/05.

DENISE JAMES AND HER FAMILY
1. "More Americans Living in Poverty," Coalition on Human Needs, 8/03.
2. Ibid.
3. Women In Prison Project, Correctional Assoc. of NY, 3/02.
4. Osborne Institute as quoted in *Justice Works: Mothers in Prison,* 4/01.
5. National Low Income Housing Coalition, 2002.
6. National Priorities Project, 1998.

RAMONA WILLIS AND THE VIRUS
1. "Revolving Door," Urban Justice Project, 2003.
2. "Children with Incarcerated Parents: An Overview of the Statistics," Child Welfare League of America.
3. WPA, "Focus on Women and Justice— Portrait of Women in Prison," 12/03.
4. U.S. Dept. of Justice Programs as quoted in *Justice Works: Mothers in Prison Fact Sheet,* 2001.
5. WPA, "Focus on Women and Justice— Portrait of Women in Prison," 12/03.

ANGELINA RIVERA—SENTENCED TO A HARD LIFE
1. U.S. Dept. of Justice Programs as quoted in *Justice Works: Mothers in Prison Fact Sheet,* 2001.
2. "Specific Needs of Women Diagnosed With Mental Illness in U.S. Jails," Bonnie Vesey, 1997.
3. "Women Offenders," Bureau of Justice Statistics, 1999.

REGINA MCKNIGHT
1. "Pregnant and Punished," by Cynthia Cooper, *Ford Foundation Report,* Winter 2003.

"Crack Baby"

There is no such thing as a "crack baby." Stories on TV and the news about the effects of crack on fetuses were unsupported, misleading and inaccurate. Dozens of studies now show that other factors are responsible for many of the problems that women who use crack are blamed for, such as poverty and lack of pre-natal care.[1]

Crack vs. Cocaine Sentencing

Crack is produced from powder cocaine. The penalties for possession or sale of crack are far more severe than for powder cocaine. A person who sells or possesses five grams of crack get the same five year federal mandatory sentence as someone who sells or possesses five hundred grams of powder cocaine. Drug policy reform advocates see these laws as racist, since 85% of people arrested for crack sale or use are Black.

Harm Reduction[2]

Harm reduction is a set of practical strategies that reduce negative consequences of drug use. It seeks to minimize the harmful effects of drug use rather than ignoring or condemning drug users. It calls for the non-judgmental, non-coercive provision of services and resources to drug users, families and communities. Needle-exchange is an example of a harm reduction strategy. Harm reduction sees drug use as a public health issue.

Mandatory Minimums

In the 1970s and 1980s, the U.S. Congress and many state legislatures passed laws that required judges to give fixed prison terms to those convicted of specific crimes, most often drug offenses. Lawmakers believed these harsh, inflexible sentencing laws would catch those at the top of the drug trade and deter others from entering it. Instead, this heavy-handed response to the nation's drug problem filled prisons with men and women found guilty low-level offences resulting prisons being filled with people serving long sentences at tremendous cost to taxpayers. Mandatory sentencing laws disproportionately affect people of color and, because of their severity, destroy families.[3]

Neoliberalism

Neoliberalism has been the dominant ideology behind economic policy for more than 20 years. Neoliberalism calls for free markets and a smaller role for the government. According to neoliberal thinking, government policies and regulations—including taxes on the wealthy—create conditions that slow down economic growth. Neoliberalism calls for free trade between the U.S. and developing countries; the reduction of protections for workers and families; the private ownership of hospitals, water, transportation and education; drastic cuts in public spending for welfare, housing and job development; and no voice for workers and unions. Neoliberalism claims its approach will generate economic growth and prosperity for all. In the neoliberal view, poverty is the result of government interference and lack of motivation on the part of poor families. However, neoliberal policies make it harder and harder for most people to survive. One way those in government and business enforce these polices is by making poor people believe they are poor because of their shortcomings rather than the effects of negative effects of neoliberal policies on their daily life.

Racialized Patriarchy

Women of color face many forms of discrimination which are deeply rooted in our society. Racialized patriarchy is what happens when racism AND sexism are combined. The effect is that the combination makes the negative effects not just two times more powerful but many more times more powerful since racism strengthens sexism and sexism strengthen racism. This powerful combination can lead women of color to face even greater vulnerability than white women to poverty, lack of access to quality education and discrimination in jobs and housing. While individual women experience its effects and individuals perpetuate it, racialized patriarchy is a complex set of harmful beliefs, attitudes, economic practices, and laws which restrict and/or prevent the full development of girls and women of color in the U.S. and around the world.

Transactional Sex

Transactional sex is the exchange of sex for money, drugs, a place to live, rent money, or what ever it is that the person performing sex needs. Many people engage in transactional sex without even realizing it. Women who engage in transactional sex by working the streets are exposed to tremendous risk of abuse and violence and exposure to sexually transmitted infections including HIV. They are also at risk of police harassment and arrest in most cities in the U.S.

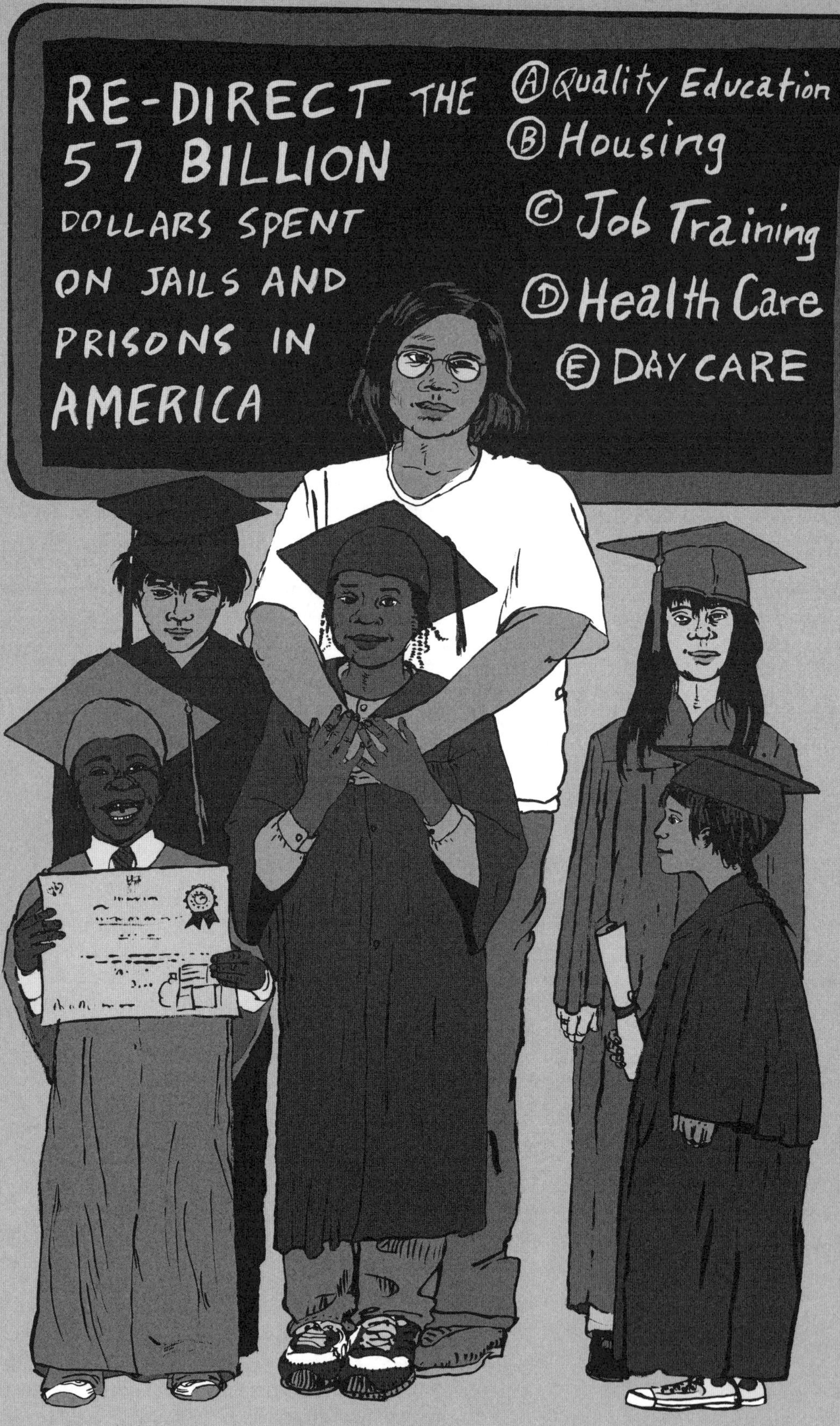
RE-DIRECT THE
57 BILLION
DOLLARS SPENT
ON JAILS AND
PRISONS IN
AMERICA
Ⓐ Quality Education
Ⓑ Housing
Ⓒ Job Training
Ⓓ Health Care
Ⓔ DAY CARE

ALSO AVAILABLE FROM PM PRESS

Diario de Oaxaca
A Sketchbook Journal of Two Years in Mexico
By Peter Kuper
ISBN: 978-1-60486-071-9
$29.95

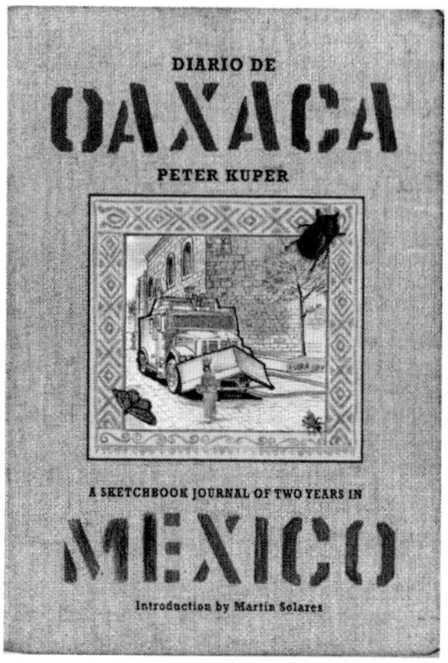

DIARIO DE
OAXACA
PETER KUPER
A SKETCHBOOK JOURNAL OF TWO YEARS IN
MEXICO
Introduction by Martín Solares

In 2006, award-winning cartoonist Peter Kuper, along with his wife and daughter, moved to the beautiful 16th century colonial town of Oaxaca, Mexico. They planned to spend a quiet year or two enjoying a different culture and getting a break from the political climate under the Bush administration. What they hadn't counted on was landing in the epicenter of Mexico's biggest political struggle in recent times.

In *Diario de Oaxaca*, Kuper employs comics, bi-lingual essays, photos, and sketches to chronicle the events that unfolded around a teacher's strike and led to a seven month siege. From the fight between strikers and government troops that left over 20 people dead, including U.S. journalist Brad Will, to explorations of the beauty of the environment, *Diario de Oaxaca* presents a unique artistic vision of life in Mexico.

"Kuper is a colossus; I have been in awe of him for over 20 years. Teachers and students everywhere take heart: Kuper has in these pages born witness to our seemingly endless struggle to educate and to be educated in the face of institutions that really don't give a damn. In this ruined age we need Kuper's unsparing compassionate visionary artistry like we need hope."
—Junot Díaz, Pulitzer Prize winning author of *The Brief Wondrous Life of Oscar Wao*

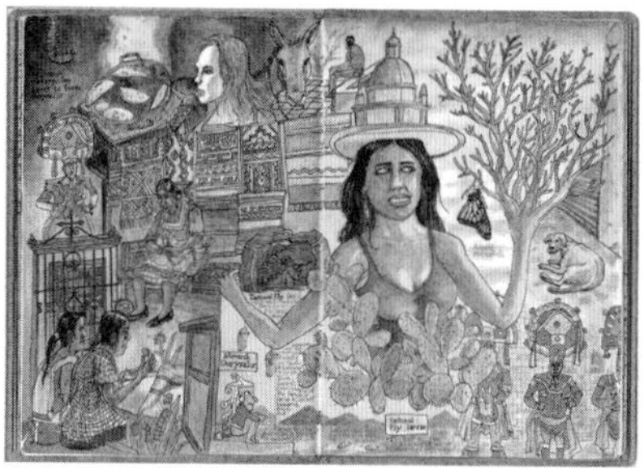

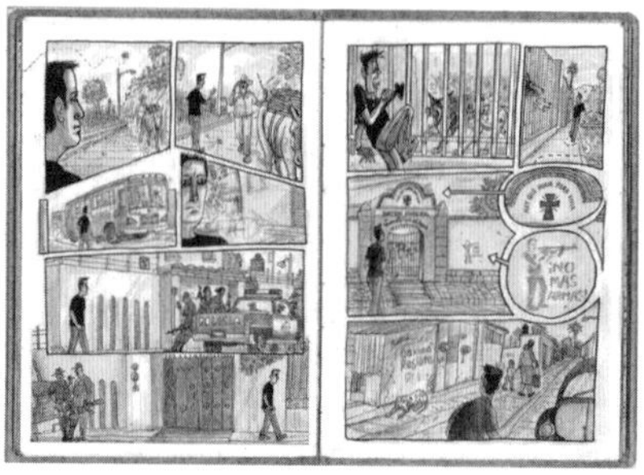

Slingshot
32 Postcards by Eric Drooker
By Eric Drooker
ISBN: 978-1-60486-016-0
$14.95

Disguised as a book of innocent postcards, Slingshot is a dangerous collection of Eric Drooker's most notorious posters. Plastered on brick walls from New York to Berlin, tattooed on bodies from Kansas to Mexico City, Drooker's graphics continue to infiltrate and inflame the body politic. Drooker is the author of two graphic novels, *Flood! A Novel in Pictures* (winner of the American Book Award), and *Blood Song: A Silent Ballad*. He collaborated with Beat poet Allen Ginsberg on the underground classic, *Illuminated Poems*. His provocative art has appeared on countless posters, book and CD covers, and his hard-edged graphics are a familiar sight on street corners throughout the world. Eric Drooker is a third generation New Yorker, born and raised on Manhattan Island. His paintings are frequently seen on covers of *The New Yorker* magazine, and hang in various art collections throughout the U.S. and Europe.

"Drooker's old Poe hallucinations of beauteous deathly reality transcend political hang-up and fix our present American dreams."
–Allen Ginsberg

"When the rush of war parades are over, a simple and elegant reminder of humanity remains—in the work of Eric Drooker."
–Sue Coe

ALSO AVAILABLE FROM PM PRESS

Signal
A Journal of International Political Graphics
Edited by Josh MacPhee and Alec "Icky" Dunn

ISBN: 978-1-60486-091-7
$14.95

ISBN: 978-1-60486-298-0
$14.95

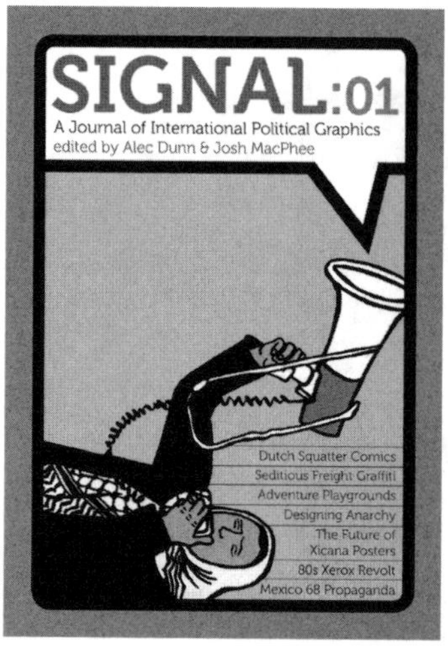
SIGNAL:01
A Journal of International Political Graphics
edited by Alec Dunn & Josh MacPhee
Dutch Squatter Comics
Seditious Freight Graffiti
Adventure Playgrounds
Designing Anarchy
The Future of Xicana Posters
80s Xerox Revolt
Mexico 68 Propaganda

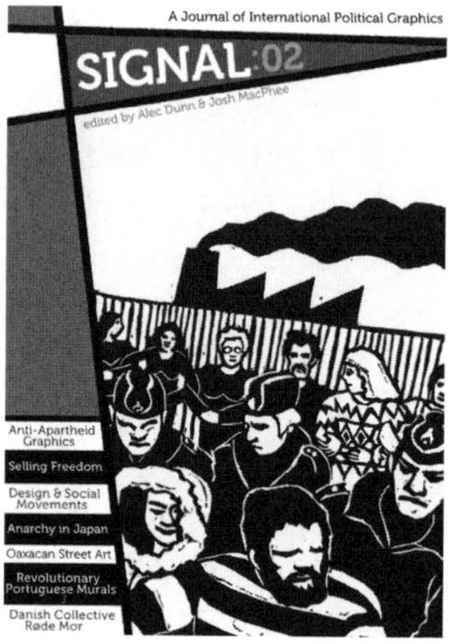
A Journal of International Political Graphics
SIGNAL:02
edited by Alec Dunn & Josh MacPhee
Anti-Apartheid Graphics
Selling Freedom
Design & Social Movements
Anarchy in Japan
Oaxacan Street Art
Revolutionary Portuguese Murals
Danish Collective Røde Mor

Signal is an ongoing book series dedicated to documenting and sharing compelling graphics, art projects, and cultural movements of international resistance and liberation struggles. Artists and cultural workers have been at the center of upheavals and revolts the world over, from the painters and poets in the Paris Commune to the poster makers and street theatre performers of the recent counter globalization movement. *Signal* will bring these artists and their work to a new audience, digging deep through our common history to unearth their images and stories. We have no doubt that *Signal* will come to serve as a unique and irreplaceable resource for activist artists and academic researchers, as well as an active forum for critique of the role of art in revolution.

In the U.S. there is a tendency to focus only on the artworks produced within our shores or from English speaking producers. *Signal* reaches beyond those bounds, bringing material produced the world over, translated from dozens of languages and collected from both the present and decades past. Although a full color printed publication, *Signal* is not limited to the graphic arts. Within its pages you will find political posters and fine arts, comics and murals, street art, site specific works, zines, art collectives, documentation of performance and articles on the often overlooked but essential role all of these have played in struggles around the world.

Signal: 01 includes:

- The Future of Xicana Printmaking: Alec Dunn and Josh MacPhee interview the Taller Tupac Amaru
- The Adventures of Red Rat: Alec Dunn interviews Johannes van de Weert
- Hard Travelin': A photo essay with IMPEACH
- Early 20th-Century Anarchist Imprints
- Mexico 68: The Graphic Production of a Movement: Santiago Armengod interviews Felipe Hernandez Moreno
- Adventure Playgrounds: A photo essay
- Designing Anarchy: Dan Poyner interviews Rufus Segar

Signal: 02 includes:

- Design, Mass-Production, and Social Movements: An Interview with Sandy K. of image-shift
- Anarchist Posters in Japan
- Breaking Chains: Political Graphics and the Anti-Apartheid Struggle
- Selling Freedom: Promotional Posters from the 1910s
- Street Art, Oaxacan Struggle, and the Mexican Context
- Covering the Wall: Revolutionary Murals in 1970s Portugal
- Røde Mor -Danish printmaking, pop music, and politics

ALSO AVAILABLE FROM PM PRESS

Revolutionary Women
A Book of Stencils
By Queen of the Neighbourhood
ISBN: 978-1-60486-200-3
$12.00

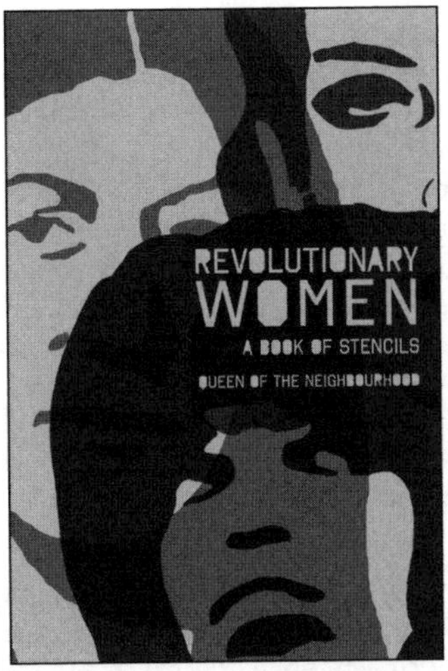
REVOLUTIONARY
WOMEN
A BOOK OF STENCILS
QUEEN OF THE NEIGHBOURHOOD

A radical feminist history and street art resource for inspired readers! This book combines short biographies with striking and usable stencil images of thirty women—activists, anarchists, feminists, freedom-fighters and visionaries.

It offers a subversive portrait history which refuses to belittle the military prowess and revolutionary drive of women, whose violent resolves often shatter the archetype of woman-as-nurturer. It is also a celebration of some extremely brave women who have spent their lives fighting for what they believe in and rallying supporters in climates where a woman's authority is never taken as seriously as a man's. The text also shares some of each woman's ideologies, philosophies, struggles and quiet humanity with quotes from their writings or speeches.

The women featured are: Harriet Tubman, Louise Michel, Vera Zasulich, Emma Goldman, Qiu Jin, Nora Connolly O'Brien, Lucia Sanchez Saornil, Angela Davis, Leila Khaled, Comandante Ramona, Phoolan Devi, Ani Pachen, Anna Mae Aquash, Hannie Schaft, Rosa Luxemburg, Brigitte Mohnhaupt, Lolita Lebron, Djamila Bouhired, Malalai Joya, Vandana Shiva, Olive Morris, Assata Shakur, Sylvia Rivera, Haydée Santamaría, Marie Equi, Mother Jones, Doria Shafik, Ondina Peteani, Whina Cooper and Lucy Parsons.

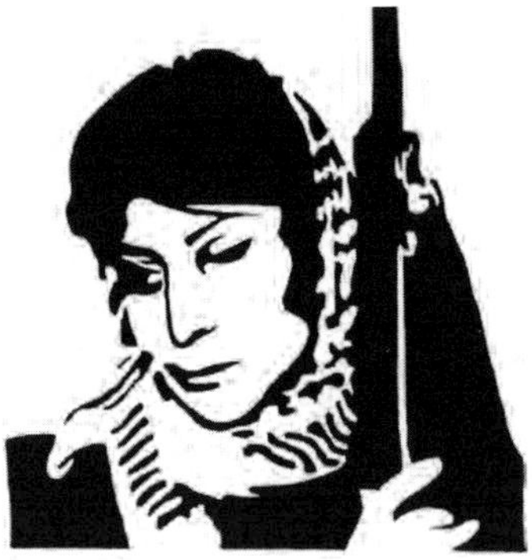
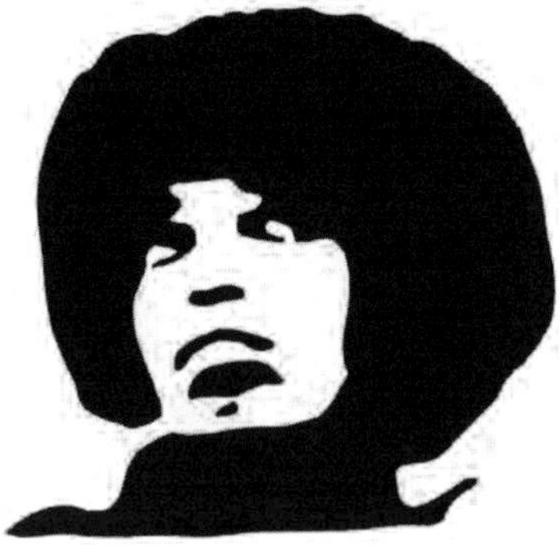
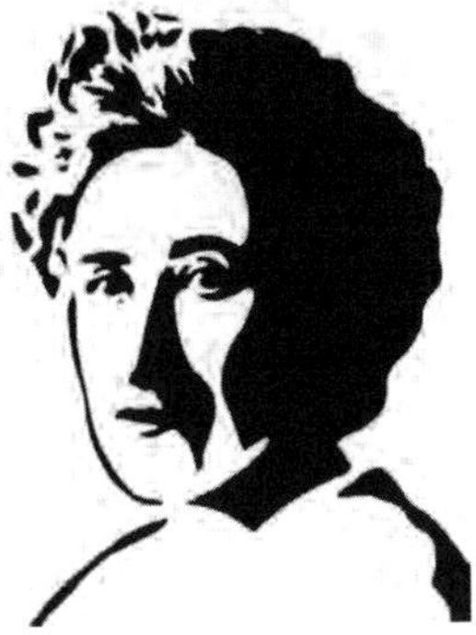

Resistance Behind Bars: The Struggles of Incarcerated Women
By Victoria Law
ISBN: 978-1-60486-018-4 • $20.00

VICTORIA LAW
RESISTANCE
BEHIND BARS
THE STRUGGLES OF INCARCERATED WOMEN

In 1974, women imprisoned at New York's maximum-security prison at Bedford Hills staged what is known as the August Rebellion. Protesting the brutal beating of a fellow prisoner, the women fought off guards, holding seven of them hostage, and took over sections of the prison.

While many have heard of the 1971 Attica prison uprising, the August Rebellion remains relatively unknown even in activist circles. Resistance Behind Bars is determined to challenge and change such oversights. As it examines daily struggles against appalling prison conditions and injustices, Resistance documents both collective organizing and individual resistance among women incarcerated in the U.S. Emphasizing women's agency in resisting the conditions of their confinement through forming peer education groups, clandestinely arranging ways for children to visit mothers in distant prisons, and raising public awareness about their lives, Resistance seeks to spark further discussion and research into the lives of incarcerated women and galvanize much-needed outside support for their struggles.

"Victoria Law's eight years of research and writing, inspired by her unflinching commitment to listen to and support women prisoners, has resulted in an illuminating effort to document the dynamic resistance of incarcerated women in the United States."
—Roxanne Dunbar-Ortiz, author of *Outlaw Woman: A Memoir of the War Years, 1960–1975*

From The Bottom of the Heap: The Autobiography of Black Panther Robert Hillary King
By Robert Hillary King
ISBN: 978-1-60486-039-9 • $24.95

FROM THE
BOTTOM
OF THE
HEAP
THE AUTOBIOGRAPHY OF BLACK PANTHER
ROBERT HILLARY KING

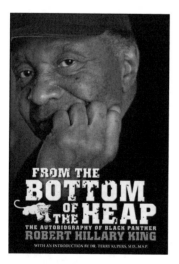

In 1970, a jury convicted Robert Hillary King of a crime he did not commit, and he was sentenced to 35 years in prison. He became a member of the Black Panther Party while in Angola State Penitentiary, successfully organizing prisoners to improve conditions. In return, prison authorities beat him, starved him, and gave him life without parole after framing him for a second crime. He was thrown into solitary confinement, where he remained in a six-by-nine-foot cell for 29 years as one of the Angola 3. In 2001, the state grudgingly acknowledged his innocence and set him free.

The conditions in Angola almost defy description, yet King never gave up his humanity, or the work towards justice for all prisoners. King's story, so simply and humbly told, strips bare the economic and social injustices inherent in our society, while being a powerful literary testimony to our own strength and capacity to overcome.

"My friendship with Robert King and the other two Angola 3 men Herman Wallace and Albert Woodfox is based on respect. These men have fought tirelessly to redress injustice, not only for themselves, but for others. This is a battle Robert is determined to win and we are determined to help him."
—Gordon Roddick, co-founder of The Body Shop

Lucasville: The Untold Story of a Prison Uprising, Second Edition
By Staughton Lynd
ISBN: 978-1-60486-224-9 $20.00

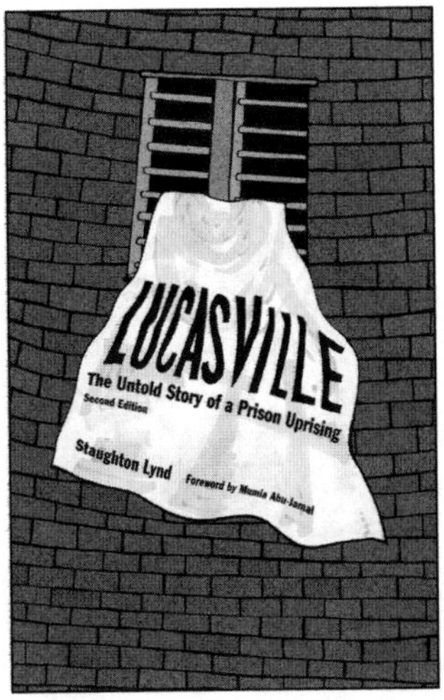
LUCASVILLE
The Untold Story of a Prison Uprising
Second Edition
Staughton Lynd
Foreword by Mumia Abu-Jamal

Lucasville tells the story of one of the longest prison uprisings in U.S. history. At the maximum-security Southern Ohio Correctional Facility in Lucasville, prisoners seized a major area of the prison on Easter Sunday, 1993. More than 400 prisoners held L block for 11 days. Nine prisoners alleged to have been informants, or "snitches," and one hostaged correctional officer were murdered.

Lucasville examines both the causes of the disturbance, what happened during the 11 days, and the fairness of the trials. Particular emphasis is placed on the interracial character of the action, as evidenced in painted slogans on walls after the surrender: "Black and White Together," "Convict Unity," and "Convict Race." An eloquent foreword by Mumia Abu-Jamal underlines these themes.

"*Lucasville* is one of the most powerful indictments of our 'justice system' I have ever read. What comes across is a litany of flaws deep in the system, and recognizably not unique to Lucasville. The detailed transcripts (yes, oral history!) give great power to the whole story."
—Howard Zinn, author of *A People's History of the United States*

Let Freedom Ring: A Collection of Documents from the Movements to Free U.S. Political Prisoners
Edited by Matt Meyer
ISBN: 978-1-60486-035-1 • $37.95

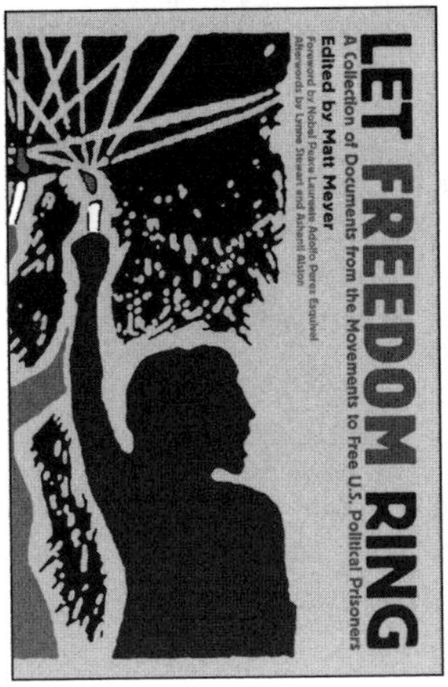
LET FREEDOM RING
A Collection of Documents from the Movements to Free U.S. Political Prisoners
Edited by Matt Meyer

Let Freedom Ring presents a two-decade sweep of essays, analyses, histories, interviews, resolutions, People's Tribunal verdicts, and poems by and about the scores of U.S. political prisoners and the campaigns to safeguard their rights and secure their freedom. In addition to an extensive section on the campaign to free death-row journalist Mumia Abu-Jamal, represented here are the radical movements that have most challenged the U.S. empire from within: Black Panthers and other Black liberation fighters, Puerto Rican independentistas, Indigenous sovereignty activists, white anti-imperialists, environmental and animal rights militants, Arab and Muslim activists, Iraq war resisters, and others.

Contributors in and out of prison (including Mumia Abu-Jamal, Dan Berger, Dhoruba Bin-Wahad, Bob Lederer, Terry Bisson, Laura Whitehorn, Safiya Bukhari, The San Francisco 8, Angela Davis, Bo Brown, Bill Dunne, Luis Nieves Falcón, Assata Shakur, Leonard Peltier, and Desmond Tutu) detail the repressive methods—from long-term isolation to sensory deprivation to politically inspired parole denial—used to attack these freedom fighters, some still caged after 30 years. This invaluable resource guide offers inspiring stories of the creative, and sometimes winning, strategies to bring them home.

About PM

PM Press was founded at the end of 2007 by a small collection of folks with decades of publishing, media, and organizing experience. PM Press co-conspirators have published and distributed hundreds of books, pamphlets, CDs, and DVDs. Members of PM have founded enduring book fairs, spearheaded victorious tenant organizing campaigns, and worked closely with bookstores, academic conferences, and even rock bands to deliver political and challenging ideas to all walks of life. We're old enough to know what we're doing and young enough to know what's at stake.

We seek to create radical and stimulating fiction and non-fiction books, pamphlets, t-shirts, visual and audio materials to entertain, educate, and inspire you. We aim to distribute these through every available channel with every available technology, whether that means you are seeing anarchist classics at our bookfair stalls; reading our latest vegan cookbook at the café; downloading geeky fiction e-books; or digging new music and timely videos from our website.

PM Press is always on the lookout for talented and skilled volunteers, artists, activists and writers to work with. If you have a great idea for a project or can contribute in some way, please get in touch.

PM Press
PO Box 23912
Oakland CA 94623
510-658-3906
www.pmpress.org

Friends of PM

These are indisputably momentous times – the financial system is melting down globally and the Empire is stumbling. Now more than ever there is a vital need for radical ideas.

In the three years since its founding – and on a mere shoestring – PM Press has risen to the formidable challenge of publishing and distributing knowledge and entertainment for the struggles ahead. With over 100 releases to date, we have published an impressive and stimulating array of literature, art, music, politics, and culture. Using every available medium, we've succeeded in connecting those hungry for ideas and information to those putting them into practice.

Friends of PM allows you to directly help impact, amplify, and revitalize the discourse and actions of radical writers, filmmakers, and artists. It provides us with a stable foundation from which we can build upon our early successes and provides a much-needed subsidy for the materials that can't necessarily pay their own way. You can help make that happen – and receive every new title automatically delivered to your door once a month – by joining as a Friend of PM Press. And, we'll throw in a free T-Shirt when you sign up.

Here are your options:
- $25 a month: Get all books and pamphlets plus 50% discount on all webstore purchases
- $25 a month: Get all CDs and DVDs plus 50% discount on all webstore purchases
- $40 a month: Get all PM Press releases plus 50% discount on all webstore purchases
- $100 a month: Superstar - Everything plus PM merchandise, free downloads, and 50% discount on all webstore purchases

For those who can't afford $25 or more a month, we're introducing **Sustainer Rates** at $15, $10 and $5. Sustainers get a free PM Press t-shirt and a 50% discount on all purchases from our website.

Your Visa or Mastercard will be billed once a month, until you tell us to stop. Or until our efforts succeed in bringing the revolution around. Or the financial meltdown of Capital makes plastic redundant. Whichever comes first.